MORE HENLEAZE CONNECTIONS:

Pastimes, Pastures and People

VERONICA BOWERMAN

ISBN 978-1-79-448830-4

DEDICATION

I would like to dedicate this book to the many local history enthusiasts who have been in touch over the years. Some have met me face to face, but others have been in contact by post or email. They have been most generous with their time and support. Their memories and paperwork have provided a rich vein of local and social history of the area in and around Henleaze for me which has resulted in five publications and two heritage trails.

Local history has enriched my life over the years through their support and friendship.

Thank you.

Veronica Bowerman

CONTENTS

ACKNOWLEDGMENTS

It is no coincidence that this latest book within the Henleaze Heritage range *MORE HENLEAZE CONNECTIONS* is being published in 2019. Included are some local history highlights on two organisations who are celebrating their centenaries.

There is also some information from individuals highlighting the latest discoveries in the area. Some of these people moved away from Henleaze many years ago but their memories have revealed some diverse and interesting social and local history connections.

So, many thanks to all our volunteers who include:

OUR CONTRIBUTORS – for providing paperwork, photos etc. that have enabled us to produce their information for others to read. Their names have been included within their respective articles.

OUR PATIENT PROOF READERS – Alan Aburrow and Caroline Sparks.

PHOTOGRAPHY EDITS – Jim Bowerman.

BOOK SUBTITLE - Duncan Ogilvie – for providing the final subtitle for this book.

COVER PHOTO - Liz Loeffler – for providing the background cover photo looking over at Old Quarry Park across Henleaze Road dual carriageway, from the former Blind School site.

Finally, my thanks and apologies if I have omitted to name you in the book if you have assisted.

CHAPTER 1 – (2019) A DUAL CENTENARY YEAR

During 1919 **Badminton School** moved to a new location on Westbury Road. The school, thanks in so small way to its founder Miriam Badock, had by then outgrown several other sites in Clifton.

In 1919 **Henleaze Swimming Club** was formed under strict Amateur Swimming Association rules. The club initially leased part of Henleaze Lake for swimming from Stanley Badock, the youngest son of Miriam Badock.

Canon Stephen Trapnell highlights the Badock family connection to these centenaries.

"I note that this year marks a DUAL centenary – and it is the 'Badock' mother and son that unites them."

Miriam Badock (nee Trapnell), the founder of Badminton School was married to William Badock. Part of their married life was spent in Southmead Manor House, close to Henleaze Lake. Their youngest son Stanley in later life became the owner of Henleaze Lake. He also lived in Holmwood House, adjacent to Badock's

Wood.

More information about both Miriam and Stanley can be found in this chapter under Badminton School.

Further details relating to Stanley can be viewed at this additional link for Henleaze Swimming Club:

http://www.henleazeswimmingclub.org/about-us/the-story-of-the-lake/

Stephen also highlights the following:

"We often used to visit Holmwood to swim in the summer, and Christmas always began with a party which included 'Handkerchief Hide & Seek' round the inside of the house."

"You will notice how Dr Sir Stanley and his mother Miriam resemble each other in their portraits a feature which Joan Badock was also to inherit."

So, if you also wish to compare:

The portrait of Miriam Badock can be found in the Badminton School chapter.

Here is a link to the portrait of Dr Sir Stanley Badock which takes pride of place in the Library of Badock Hall at the University of Bristol: **http://www.fobw.org.uk**

∧∧∧∧∧∧∧∧∧∧∧∧∧∧∧∧∧∧∧∧∧∧∧∧∧∧∧∧∧∧

BADMINTON SCHOOL - CENTENARY IN WESTBURY ON TRYM

THE ENTRANCE ON WESTBURY ROAD IS FAMILIAR – BUT WHAT LIES INSIDE? (2017 PHOTO)

Introduction

Badminton School educates girls to thrive in a rapidly evolving, fast moving and increasingly complex world. They have always been proud to welcome pupils of many nationalities from all over the world. They are also a sizeable day school, attracting pupils from local families and junior schools.

A lively outreach programme sees girls visiting local primary schools to demonstrate science experiments, or help with reading, and they frequently welcome groups on-site to share their sporting facilities or enjoy themed days sampling our outstanding teaching.

Their Christmas Bazaars and traditional Summer Fêtes are much enjoyed by the local community. As a result of a generous bursary and scholarship programme Badminton education can be available to girls from all sections of the community (*See their website*

Miriam Badock (nee Trapnell) 30 July, 1831 – 12 June, 1915)

Miriam Badock started Badminton School in 1858 in a respectable suburban stone villa in Burlington Road, just off Whiteladies Road, in Redland.

(MIRIAM KNEW HOW TO DRESS AND ALWAYS WORE BEAUTIFUL CLOTHES. SHE WAS ALSO ENCOURAGED TO DO SO BY HER HUSBAND WILLIAM)

^^^^^^^^^^^^^^^^^^^^^^^^^^^^^^^^^^^

(1858 - EARLY 1890s) MRS MIRIAM BADOCK

LOCAL RESIDENT, FOUNDER AND FIRST HEAD OF BADMINTON SCHOOL

Badminton School's founder was Mrs Miriam Badock, a mother with four very young children. Miriam was born Miriam Trapnell, and her father Henry owned a very well-known Bristol furniture and cabinet makers which had its own factory, branches throughout Bristol and head office on College Green. Trapnell's later became Trapnell and Gane, and after Miriam's father's death his partner P.E. Gane continued to run the business, until the destruction of its College Green premises and St Paul's factory during the Second World War contributed to its decline and eventual closure in 1956.

Most of Miriam's 11 siblings were boys. The three daughters were worshipped by their father, Henry but, sadly, Miriam's elder sister, Mary Ann died as a toddler, leaving her and younger sister, Milly as the only daughters. Several of the boys did not survive childhood either.

From her early teens Miriam attended Miss Thompson's School, a large school on St Michael's Hill with an excellent reputation gained through forward thinking teaching and strict rules. Miriam was a quick and clever girl, but in those days, there were no examinations. By the time Miriam had completed the curriculum neither of her parents felt comfortable about leaving their attractive young daughter at home each day. Both parents, at this time, were working for the company business which had expanded rapidly. So, Henry Trapnell asked Miss Thompson to keep his daughter on longer, but Miss Thompson said it would not be suitable for her to go over the syllabus again. However, it was agreed that Miriam could stay on and study Greek instead which she really enjoyed. After these additional studies were completed and Miriam was back home it was also decided that her mother would leave the business altogether to manage their home at

Victoria Lodge, in Whiteladies Road.

Caleb Trapnell, one of Miriam's older brothers. worked as a designer in the family business. When William Badock came down from London to see him in about 1851, Caleb asked their parents if they could put him up for the night at Victoria Lodge.

Miriam would have been about 19 or 20 then. William and Miriam got on very well from this first meeting at the Trapnell's home and within six months were engaged over a game of chess. Miriam's parents later moved to Oakfield Road and William and Miriam were married at Clifton Parish Church in 1852. Her wedding dress was white moire antique, trimmed with ermine. They lived in London initially as William's business was in Clapham.

Miriam had three babies rather quickly named Walter, Will and Gertie. Shortly after this time, when William was riding, he was thrown from his horse breaking a leg and subsequently developing a kidney problem. His condition worsened and, as he was not able to work, money was not coming in from the business. Miriam wrote to her parents asking for advice. Her father told her to *'Pack up everything you've got. Come down to Bristol all of you. I have a house I can put you into and I think I have got a business William could take.'*

Miriam and William and family moved into Burlington Road, off Whiteladies Road, Bristol. William took over the cabinet making business which thrived, but his health continued to be a problem. They found that they were still unable to generate enough income to cover their needs. By 1858, with Miriam expecting their fourth child in June, they decided to look at other ways of increasing their income. A paying guest, Miss Holborrow was taken in and, almost immediately, became a very good and supportive friend to Miriam.

When William's health worsened Miriam was able to talk over her worries with Miss Holborrow who enabled her to focus on her own talents. Although Miriam could not initially see a way forward with three young children as well as a sick husband, Miss Holborrow, a few days later, mentioned that she had just received a letter from her sister, Mrs Hillier, who had three young girls. She was keen for her children to have a good education and thought that Miriam might be able to help. With great fortitude and enterprise, Miriam Badock had now identified her most marketable asset, her education at Miss Thompson's school at Campden House, St Michael's Hill, Bristol, which had been unusually good for a 19th century daughter. William, was not at all keen for Miriam to start such a venture but, he agreed that if her mother thought it was a good idea, he would go along with it.

Later when Miriam visited her mother; like William, she was not happy with the idea. However, she did agree to talk to Miriam's father later. Her father subsequently said *'I think, my dear, the Lord helps those who help themselves and if you take these three and teach them you shall have your little sister Milly for a fourth.'* (Miriam's sister was 12 years younger than she was.) He continued: *'Your children shan't suffer. I'll pay for a good nurse for the children. They will be all right.'* Miriam was thrilled with these offers and ran home to William to talk it over. It was agreed that the school should start on 1 August, 1858 following the birth of the new baby, Herbert on 15 June 1858. In those days there were no terms – just two half years – the first one beginning 1 August and finishing in the middle of December and the second from the beginning of January or February. There were breaks of a few days each for Michaelmas and Easter.

On 1 August, 1858 the school opened with seven children including Pidgie. Her parents, the Parnalls, had to unexpectedly return to Demerara, then part of British Guiana. Mrs Parnall had previously called on Miriam to ask for information about Miss Thompson. They wanted Pidgie to be educated to the same high standards that Miss Thompson offered but since Miriam attended her school she had died. Pidgie was nine years old, used to having her own way and had been brought up by black servants. Although she was quite a handful Miriam grew very fond of her over the years. Pidgie stayed on until she was 18 but during those nine years never saw her parents.

Miriam Badock's little school thrived at Burlington Road so larger premises were soon needed. The school moved to 1 Berkeley Square and extra staff were taken on to cope with the growing number of pupils. With this continuing increase of pupils, a move to 31 Berkeley Square was soon needed. Five years later, after Herbert's arrival, Edith Mary was born at 31 Berkeley Square in 1863. However, Miriam had fallen downstairs and landed at the bottom just a month before the birth. They were all very worried about her and brought her bed down to the drawing room where she stayed until Edith Mary was born. The remaining children were all born during the school holidays when Miriam was Head. Edith Mary was followed by Percy and then Stanley (Sir Stanley Badock), the youngest.

Everything was going really well, but then a Mrs Hill wrote saying that she had two little girls that she wanted to send there the next term. Miriam was pleased to have two more boarders but then she received a telegram asking if the daughters could be received at once. Miriam telegraphed back 'With pleasure.' When the children arrived one of the Governesses showed the children their rooms and helped them to unpack and settle in. However, the Governess thought it unusual that all the children's clothes were brand new and reported this to Miriam. When the two children went to bed that evening, they complained that they were not feeling well. The next morning one of them was very ill indeed so Miriam arranged for a doctor to call to see them. He said they both had scarlet fever; then sadly, the two Hill children died. When Mr and Mrs Hill arrived for the funeral of the children Mrs Hill said *'Mrs Badock, will you ever forgive me? I thought to save my children. I had one child lying dead at home and I thought I could send them straight off to you. So, I sent them to London and had them completely outfitted at a London shop and thought everything would be all right.'*

Miriam was at her wit's end and so decided to break up the school. Pidgie was looked after by Miriam's mother and all the others were sent home. William decided that it was necessary to disinfect the house and to temporarily relocate his family to rented accommodation, believed to be in Portishead. They had not been there for more than a couple of days when William and son Will developed scarlet fever but fortunately, they recovered. It was fearful blow to Miriam at the time, but she learnt many lessons from it.

Fortunately, Miriam was able to restart the school soon after 31 Berkeley Square was disinfected but, by 1870, owing to its continuing popularity the school needed bigger premises again. William and Miriam agreed to purchase Badminton House, Worcester Terrace, Clifton. The previous occupant had been an old clergyman who took in noblemen. One of these was the Duke of Beaufort's son, the Marquis of Worcester. The clergyman was so proud of this that he named the house Badminton House after the Duke's estate. Many people could not understand why William and Miriam had decided on an area which, at that time, was quite out of the way. However, the school continued to grow with more day pupils.

Daughter, Edith Mary Badock recalled when they first moved to Badminton House around 1870 there was no room in the bedrooms for the crinolines so nails were driven into the walls in a long passage outside and the girls took off their crinolines and hung them up here. The school continued at Worcester Terrace for many years before settling on its location at Westbury on Trym in 1919. Edith Mary Badock had, during these years, married Henry Caleb Trapnell from their Worcester Terrace home and school where she also taught after her marriage.

UCLES – University of Cambridge Local Examination Syndicate for school leaving exams had chosen Bristol as one of its centres for boys in 1858. By 1868 the Committee who ran these examinations proposed that girls should also be included. Several members of the Bristol Committee called on Miriam wanting to know if she would be willing to put pupils in for the exam. They advised costs, how it would be done, and the desirability of girls also achieving this standard. It was considered a most advanced and dangerous thing to do but there was great excitement about it. After reviewing all the particulars Miriam put it to the girls and seven volunteers came forward. Every one of them passed. It was a great feather in their cap for Badmintonians who were among the earliest female students to gain such a qualification.

In 1892, Maud Everett was first Badminton girl to study medicine, winning a place at the London School of Medicine for Women.

During her time as Head, Miriam had given birth to three more children, all in the school holidays, before retiring in the 1890s.

(EARLY 1890S–1911) MISS ELLEN BARTLETT

BADMINTON'S SECOND HEAD

After Mrs Miriam Badock retired in the early 1890s, the School was taken over by a colleague and ex-pupil, Miss Ellen Bartlett, and her two sisters. The School continued to expand, taking over a number of houses in Worcester Terrace, Clifton until in 1911 when Miss Beatrice May Baker (known as BMB) was appointed Headmistress.

(1911-1947) MISS BEATRICE MAY BAKER (KNOWN AS BMB)

BADMINTON'S THIRD HEAD

Fiercely intellectual and politically something of a radical, under BMB's leadership Badminton was soon gaining not just a national but also an international reputation.

As Miss Baker began to draw on her extensive list of contacts in cultural, philosophical and political circles she provided Badminton girls with unusually diverse opportunities to learn more about the world around them.

In 1919 the beautiful Cote Bank estate in the suburb of Westbury-on-Trym was put up for sale.

Badminton House, Junior School, Westbury-on-Trym.

BADMINTON HOUSE SCHOOL

Shrewdly Miss Baker took the great financial gamble of purchasing the site and little by little the School moved to its present campus in the early 1920s. Modern facilities were created in new, purpose-built buildings and the historic great house, Northcote, and its satellite farm buildings, stables and coach house were all sympathetically adapted. In 1933 the School was made a Public School with a Board of Governors and the Academic House system was introduced.

Thanks to the farm's sheep-dip, Badminton was one of the first girls' schools to boast its very own on-site swimming pool!

THE FORMER SHEEP DIP POOL

Between the wars, BMB and her fiercely intellectual cohort of staff forged a school with a world-wide reputation. Girls and staff had opportunities to take foreign trips and went on exchanges, visited the League of Nations headquarters in Switzerland (the precursor to the United Nations) and the School attracted pupils from India, Burma, West Africa and the West Indies. Thanks to BMB's Quaker contacts, during the 1930s a number of European Jewish refugee children fleeing from Nazi persecution were taken into the School community.

As the Second World War increased in ferocity, in 1940 Bristol was heavily bombed and the decision was taken to evacuate the School to the Tors Hotel, in Lynmouth, North Devon, although some of the younger Junior pupils remained in Bristol. Intellectual standards were never compromised in spite of the School's geographical isolation, and Miss Baker organised visits and lectures by many distinguished writers, artists and politicians.

1942 - HALF TERM SUMMER RAMBLE IN DEVON

Meanwhile in Bristol the campus was occupied by American troops preparing for D-Day, and when the girls returned from Devon, they found Bren gun carriers had been driven across the lawns and a large Nissan hut built on the playing field.

B.M.B. with the staff 'cleaners' at Cote Grange, Easter 1945.

1945 - RESTORING SCHOOL READY FOR THE SUMMER TERM

The staff, joined by a dedicated band of Old Girls and parents, spent the Easter vacation of 1945 restoring the premises back into a respectable state ready for the start of the Summer Term in April.

After successfully master-minding the return to Bristol, Miss Baker retired.

BMB lived in Northcote House for much of her tenure as Headmistress and even after retirement continued to live on-site in a commodious house, at the bottom of Cote Lane, which is still part of the Badminton campus today.

Many of BMB's dedicated staff were also residents of Henleaze and Westbury, living on campus or in one of the many satellite houses owned by the School over the years in Great Brockeridge, Downs Road and Westbury Road.

∧∧∧∧∧∧∧∧∧∧∧∧∧∧∧∧∧∧∧∧∧∧∧∧∧∧∧∧∧∧∧∧∧∧∧∧∧∧

(1919-1923) MR AND MRS LYN HARRIS

In 1919 the Heads of Badminton Junior School, Mr Lyn Harris and his wife, Eleanor, moved to the Northcote estate while the Seniors remained in Clifton as facilities were built or modified. Lyn Harris was a remarkable – some might say notorious – figure who was a Quaker, a Cambridge graduate and pacifist who had been imprisoned as a conscientious objector during the First World War. The couple moved on when the Seniors relocated to Westbury in 1923 and the schools reunited.

One of the Badminton Junior School's academic Houses is still named Harris, and he continued to serve as a Badminton Governor for many years.

WW1 conscientious objectors like Lyn Harris faced ridicule and worse.

This image courtesy of
https://www.worldwar1postcards.com/

^^^^^^^^^^^^^^^^^^^^^^^^^^^^^^^^^^

(1947-1966) MISS BRENDA SANDERSON (KNOWN AS BMS)

BADMINTON'S FOURTH HEAD

Miss Brenda Sanderson (BMS), was a passionate believer in girls' education and boarding.

The School celebrated its one hundredth birthday in 1958 with the construction of a new Science Block (opened by Countess Mountbatten of Burma) and a cantata commissioned from celebrated musician Sir Michael Tippett, who returned in the early 1980s to open the new purpose-built Music School which still bears his name.

Miss Sanderson continued the international outlook of Miss Baker, and the School both attended and hosted meetings of internationally minded schools. She also recognised the importance of physical education, and the Gymnasium was opened in 1965. Miss Sanderson retired in 1966.

(1966-1969) MISS JOANNA PIERCY - BADMINTON'S FIFTH HEAD

Miss Sanderson's successor, Miss Joanna Piercy left after three years to get married.

However, at the end of January 2012, well-known artist Lucy Willis, an Old Girl of the school, presented her portrait of ex-headmistress Joanna Turner (nee Piercy) to the Headmistress of the day, Mrs Jan Scarrow.

Lucy Willis had been commissioned by the OBA and the Governors to paint the portrait in order to complete the gallery of ex Head Teachers of the school which can be found displayed in Northcote. For more details of Lucy's work see her website http://www.lucywillis.com/

^^^^^^^^^^^^^^^^^^^^^^^^^^^^^^^^^^^^^

(1969-1981) MISS CLARE HARVEY - BADMINTON'S SIXTH HEAD

Miss Harvey oversaw an increase in the numbers of students from abroad and believed the School needed a purpose-built Sixth Form Centre. (The above photo from school archives was taken for a magazine feature by the school during the early 1970s.)

The new Sixth Form Centre - like the new Library – was designed by celebrated architect Sir Hugh Casson. It was one of the first Sixth Form Centres in an independent school in the UK and reflecting the growing trend towards creating a different way of learning and living for post-16 students. It was opened by the Duchess of Kent. It was further extended in the 1990s with the growth and popularity of Sixth Form study in the school and increasing numbers applying.

^^

(1981-1997) MR CLIFFORD GOULD – BADMINTON'S SEVENTH HEAD

Clifford Gould was appointed Headmaster in 1981 amidst a mass of publicity, as one of the first male Heads of an all-girls' school in the UK. He was passionate about both appointing teachers who were inspirational and the importance of educating girls for their future careers. He oversaw an extension to the Science Block. In 1984 a covered and heated 25m swimming pool was built on the site of the old open-air pool, but Mr Gould's major project was the building of a new contemporary Creative Arts Centre, which was opened in 1994 by former pupil and leading British novelist and philosopher Dame Iris Murdoch.

Mr Gould continued the tradition of internationalism by setting up links with Model United Nations (MUN) and the European Youth Parliament (EYP). Pupil numbers climbed ever-higher as Badminton's reputation as a world-class centre of education for girls continued to grow.

∧∧∧∧∧∧∧∧∧∧∧∧∧∧∧∧∧∧∧∧∧∧∧∧∧∧∧∧∧∧∧∧∧

(1997-2012) MRS JAN SCARROW - BADMINTON'S EIGHTH HEAD

2008 was the 150th anniversary of Badminton School. During that year the Casson Library was upgraded as part of the Sanderson House project and campus development. This new boarding house, Sanderson was named after former Headmistress Miss Brenda Sanderson. It demonstrated the School's belief in and commitment to boarding and girls' education.

Jan retired in July 2012 after 15 highly successful years. (Photo courtesy of Jan Scarrow)

^^^^^^^^^^^^^^^^^^^^^^^^^^^^^^^^^^

(2012 TO DATE) MRS REBECCA TEAR - BADMINTON'S NINTH HEAD

Mrs Rebecca Tear became Head in 2012, bringing a youthful vitality and vigour, and determined to review every aspect of the Badminton community. Like the founder of Badminton School, Mrs Badock, she combines a very demanding professional life with being a wife and mother, and as such is an outstanding role model for her students.

As well as leading the School through a highly successful ISI Inspection in 2015 which saw the School rated as Excellent in all areas, Mrs Tear has continued to modernise and extend the campus and its facilities, culminating this year in master-minding, with the Governors, a new purpose-built Sports Centre, reflecting the School's commitment to sport and fitness.

Also, academically excelling, as in 2018 the school was the highest ranked school in the South West according to the Times and Telegraph GCSE league tables.

In cherishing the School's internationalism, commitment to girls' education and their moral, physical, spiritual and emotional wellbeing, Mrs Tear is preserving the Badminton legacy and creating a School which prepares girls for whatever the 21st Century may bring.

∧∧∧∧∧∧∧∧∧∧∧∧∧∧∧∧∧∧∧∧∧∧∧∧∧∧∧∧∧∧∧∧

THE BADOCK, TRAPNELL AND GANE FAMILIES

THE TRAPNELL CONNECTION

The Founder of Badminton School, Mrs Miriam Badock was born Miriam Trapnell, daughter of Henry Trapnell who owned a fashionable and successful Bristol cabinet makers. In later life Henry and his sons were joined in business by a partner, and the company became Trapnell and Gane.

After Henry's death Mr P E Gane and his son continued the business from 1909 until the destruction of its flagship store on College Green and its St Paul's factory during the Second World War hastened its demise in 1954.

C1910s TRAPNELL & GANE. THEIR SHOP ON COLLEGE GREEN

∧∧∧∧∧∧∧∧∧∧∧∧∧∧∧∧∧∧∧∧∧∧∧∧∧∧∧∧∧∧∧∧

SIR STANLEY BADOCK (1867-1945)

The legacy of the Non-Conformist Badock's, who worshipped at Highbury Congregational Chapel (now Cotham Parish Church), and the Quaker Gane family, continues to be felt today. Civic minded and charitable in their outlook, both families have left an indelible mark.

Miriam and William's youngest son was Sir Stanley Badock (1867-1945). He was a Director of Capper Pass & Son Ltd, who were metal refiners with a smelting works in Bedminster, and was also Sheriff of Bristol from 1908 to 1909 and the Founder and Chairman of the Bristol Civic League of Social Service.

From 1922 to 1945 he was Pro-chancellor of Bristol University and Chairman of The University of Bristol Council from its foundation in 1918 until 1943. He was knighted in 1943 and died in December 1945. He lived at Holmwood, Westbury-on-Trym and is the Badock in whose honour Badock Hall, one of Bristol University's Halls of Residence across the Downs, is named. He also donated Bristol University's magnificent ceremonial silver mace.

In 1937, Sir Stanley gave part of his Holmwood estate to Bristol Corporation so that the citizens of Bristol could enjoy what is now known as Badock's Wood as a public open space in perpetuity. The wood adjoined his home, Holmwood House and his parents' home, Southmead House.

BADOCK'S WOOD

In 1872 the joint estates of the Llewellin family (Holmwood House and Southmead Manor) were bought and owned by Henry Green from 1872 to 1924. In 1871 the last of the Llewellins – Richard 111, a bachelor had died. The estate included an abandoned quarry which, by 1911, had become a lake. Mr Green leased the lake to Dr Badock who stocked it for fishing. Dr Badock or Mr Green leased part of it to Mr Sidney Curtis who admitted the public for bathing. The lake had previously been run by others for swimming purposes including a Mr Weeks before Sidney and later the swimming club leased it. From 1919 lake was then leased by Dr Badock to the newly established Henleaze Swimming Club. In 1924 Dr Badock purchased the estate and continued to lease the lake to the Swimming Club. He subsequently sold the Lake to them in 1933. Sir Stanley died in 1945.

∧∧∧∧∧∧∧∧∧∧∧∧∧∧∧∧∧∧∧∧∧∧∧∧∧∧∧∧∧∧∧∧∧∧

THE GANE LEGACY

The Gane Trust was created in Bristol in 1954 after the furniture business was wound up, by P.E. Gane's son, Crofton Gane (1877-1967). Under Crofton's Quaker-inspired leadership, Gane's became a model for benign worker/employer relations - as early as 1935 a bonus scheme and medical scheme were introduced, which included share allotments for the workers. A pioneering Modernist furniture designer and manufacturer, Crofton had joined the family firm in 1896, served in the Friends' Ambulance Division in the First World War, returned to Bristol and became passionate about the new modern spirit in design, founding a Bristol branch of the newly formed Design and Industries Association.

Today, The Trust's principal activity is a general grant application scheme to support individuals engaged in the crafts, design, the arts or social care and welfare. They have a particular remit for the South West of England, but also accept applications from all over the United Kingdom. Its headquarters is in Park Row.

∧∧∧∧∧∧∧∧∧∧∧∧∧∧∧∧∧∧∧∧∧∧∧∧∧∧∧∧∧∧∧∧

SOME FORMER PUPILS

JOSEPH COOPER

The Harris's (heads of Badminton Junior School 1919-1923) were recalled by celebrated classical musician and broadcaster Joseph Cooper, who hosted the popular classical music quiz *Face the Music* for the BBC between 1966 and 1979. Born at Southdene, Southfield Road, Westbury-on-Trym, Cooper began his education at Badminton, which in those days accepted little boys into its kindergarten.

Joseph's mother was shocked and outraged when she found the socialist principles of Lyn Harris extended to expecting the children to clear away and wash their own dishes after lunch. He told Mrs Cooper that he believed all children should be treated alike and taught to be useful, and he did not believe in class distinctions. Fortunately, the excellence of the school in all other respects quelled Mrs Cooper's wrath and Joseph remained there until it was time for him to move to a preparatory school prior to applying to Clifton College.

Joseph Cooper hosted celebrity guests such as Joyce Grenfell and Richard Attenborough on his BBC quiz show *Face the Music*. His autobiography was published in 1979.

For more information about Joseph Cooper see: **https://en.wikipedia.org/wiki/Joseph_Cooper_(broadcaster)**

^^^^^^^^^^^^^^^^^^^^^^^^^^^^^^^^^^^^^

IRIS MURDOCH AND INDIRA NEHRU (LATER GANDHI)

Between the first and second world wars, BMB and her fiercely intellectual cohort of staff forged a school with a world-wide reputation. Girls and staff had opportunities to take foreign trips and went on exchanges, visited the League of Nations headquarters in Switzerland (the precursor to the United Nations) and the School attracted pupils from India, Burma, West Africa and the West Indies. Thanks to BMB's Quaker contacts, during the 1930s a number of European Jewish refugee children fleeing from Nazi persecution were taken into the School community.

In 1937, Badminton School organised a peace conference, which was reported on by former pupil Iris Murdoch. Indira Nehru (later Gandhi) who was then in the Sixth Form, spoke about India – the country of which she was later to become Prime Minister.

For further information -

Iris Murdoch – **https:/en.wikipedia.org/wiki/Iris_Murdoch**

Indira Gandhi – **https://en.wikipedia.org/wiki/Indira_Gandhi**

^^^^^^^^^^^^^^^^^^^^^^^^^^^^^^^^^^^

CHARLOTTE LESLIE

One of Clifford Gould's pupils was local day girl Charlotte Leslie, daughter of a surgeon at Southmead Hospital and the BRI. Charlotte proved herself not only a gifted Classics student but a swimmer of considerable potential. The study won out over the poolside, and she read Classics at Balliol College, Oxford.

After the 9/11 terrorist attack Charlotte felt she had to make a difference to the world and began a successful but ultimately unfulfilling media career. She began to play an active part in politics, and in 2010 was selected by the Conservative Party as candidate for Bristol North-West and was duly elected to Parliament at the age of thirty-one, making her one of the youngest MPs in Parliament. She achieved a swing of 8.86% from the incumbent Labour candidate.

Charlotte based her constituency office on the Henleaze Road and worked tirelessly for the people of North-West Bristol, but was one of the casualties of the General Election called by Theresa May in 2017 maintaining her vote but losing out to Labour's Darren Jones.

Charlotte subsequently left Bristol to be with her new work in London as Director of the Conservative Middle East Council.

'I'd been interested in the Middle East from 9/11, which propelled me indirectly into politics, so something of a full circle! I do however miss the very many wonderful friends I made in BNW in my time as MP (and dropping in for a pint at The Mouse!)'

Photo 2014 – courtesy of Charlotte Leslie - taken at Westbury on Trym Church of England School

ΛΛΛΛΛΛΛΛΛΛΛΛΛΛΛΛΛΛΛΛΛΛΛΛΛΛΛΛΛΛΛΛΛ

FORMER TEACHER

MISS E C (LISALOTTE) LESCHKE

Another long-time resident of Henleaze was Miss Leschke who taught German at Badminton before and after the second world war, finally retiring to her house in Henleaze in 1974. Although very frail in her later years, she could often be seen travelling around Henleaze in her small electric mobility vehicle until her death in the early 2000s.

After finishing school in the 1930s, she had come to England to improve her English and spent a year teaching and caring for borders at Badminton before starting her degree course at Bristol University. As her mother was Jewish, it was clear she could not return to Germany and in 1940 she took up a permanent position at Badminton and helped organise the evacuation to Lynmouth.

After the war she travelled to Geneva in 1949 with Miss Sanderson and with other like-minded educationalists, who met to set up the CIS - Conference of Internationally-Minded Schools under the auspices of UNESCO. This led to Badminton hosting International Festival of the Arts in 1950. In the 1960s she became very committed to working with Save the Children. She used to lament that if only she had been more alert, she could have changed the course of history: sometime in the 1930s she had been looking over the railings as she stood on the upper deck of a ferry, watching other passengers boarding, and recognised Adolph Hitler amongst them! If only she had had something heavy, and the presence of mind to drop it.

∧∧∧∧∧∧∧∧∧∧∧∧∧∧∧∧∧∧∧∧∧∧∧∧∧∧∧∧∧∧∧∧∧

(OBA) OLD BADMINTONIAN ASSOCIATION

The OBA was started in 1911 and Old Girls have stayed in regular contact with each other and the School ever since. In Miss Baker's day, they would enjoy a whole weekend of events annually and Miss Baker clearly devoted a great deal of energy and thought into her address each year, reminding OBs of the School's values and urging them in the troubled 1930s and 40s to work for peace and support international movements such as the League of Nations.

Old Girls also enjoyed reunions and 'at homes' hosted by members although more recently the increasingly busy lives of women have made events hosted by the School in Westbury-on-Trym or at venues in London more practical. We have also held regular reunions and receptions abroad, most recently in Hong Kong, Lagos and Dubai. Old Badmintonians frequently drop by when passing through Bristol and love sharing their higher education experiences and professional expertise with current pupils through talks, seminars or informal meetings.

Many OBs of all ages and generations make special efforts to attend the School's annual summer celebrations when year group reunions often feature. The generosity and supportiveness shown by Old Badmintonians to each other and to the School show how close the bonds formed by shared childhood and adolescent experiences remain.

^^^^^^^^^^^^^^^^^^^^^^^^^^^^^^^^^^^

FINAL THOUGHTS

This project, was initiated to celebrate the 100th anniversary of the move of Badminton School from Clifton to Westbury on Trym.

We have attempted to give readers an overview of a unique historic school through this edition of *More Henleaze Connections.*

We know there are many other pupils and staff that could have been included. So, if there is anyone you personally would like to highlight any of them please email Badminton archives:

oba@badmintonschool.co.uk with details together with any relevant photos.

Photos, where not acknowledged, are from Badminton School archives.

Many thanks to Wikipedia for providing links containing additional information on many of the former Badminton pupils highlighted in this article. Wikipedia is a multilingual, web-based, free encyclopaedia based on a model of openly editable content. It is the largest and most popular general reference work on the Internet.

For more information about them see:

https://en.wikipedia.org/wiki/Main_Page

EDITOR'S NOTE: During this project I have realised that Miriam Badock was an amazing woman. It is pleasing to see that her legacy has been passed on and that Badminton School continues to go from strength to strength.

Many thanks, particularly to Old Girl, Rebecca Robertson, for giving me access to information from the School archives, including the letter from Stephen Trapnell, the great grandson of Henry Trapnell plus detailed notes compiled by Edith Mary Trapnell (nee Badock) 1863-1954, Miriam and William Badock's second daughter who married Henry Caleb Trapnell. The guidance from Natasha Bishop was also really helpful in completing this project. I wish the school an enjoyable and well-deserved centenary. See link:

https://www.badmintonschool.co.uk/

∧∧∧∧∧∧∧∧∧∧∧∧∧∧∧∧∧∧∧∧∧∧∧∧∧∧∧∧∧∧∧∧∧∧

HENLEAZE SWIMMING CLUB CENTENARY 2019

HENLEAZE BATHING LAKE, WESTBURY ON TRYM.

HENLEAZE LAKE, MAY 1915 - PICTURE COURTESY OF THE CLUB

Henleaze Swimming Club will be celebrating its centenary in 2019 and is currently planning what this will involve.

A key element of the celebrations will be the publication of a new book about the Lake in May 2019. Local author Susie Parr (The Story of Swimming) has undertaking the mammoth task of going through 100 years of club papers and minutes. Many interesting facts and stories about the Lake have emerged. For instance, swimming started at the Lake much earlier than had been previously thought, with evidence of swimming and ice skating from about 1907.

The Club has also collected many new photographs of the Lake from 1910 onwards that will be included in the new book. The Club is still collecting people's memories and photographs of the Lake. If you have any, please contact the Lake via the Club's website:

www.henleazeswimmingclub.org The Club's History Group would be very pleased to hear from you.

.

CHAPTER 2 - PEOPLE & PROPERTIES

CHARLES DICKENS

Dickens as a shorthand Parliamentary Reporter on The Morning Chronicle was often sent to report on news items first hand including the Bristol Riots in 1831.

Pickwick Papers – published 1836 – mentions Bristol in Chapters, 14,37,38,39,47,48 and 50.

Barnaby Rudge (chapter 81) – Published 1840-41 and Bleak House (chapter 6) published in instalments during 1852 and 53 also make brief reference to Bristol.

It would seem that Dickens had some knowledge of the city from his visits here – perhaps, initially, from his time during the Bristol Riots in 1831?

The Victoria Rooms, Clifton, built in 1841, played host to many a literary icon. Charles Dickens and his friend Wilkie Collins performed two plays here in 1851.

BYLANES OFF EASTFIELD

BYLANES - Pickwick Papers, written by Charles Dickens, clearly outlines the property Bylanes, adjacent to the land on which Amelia Edwards' house was built in Eastfield. (Amelia Edwards was a renowned Victorian Egyptologist:

see **https://www.ees.ac.uk/**)

The name of the house can still be clearly seen on the right-hand pillar of this photo from the Sylvia Kelly collection.

Charles Dickens may possibly have known of Amelia Edwards through his friend and illustrator George Cruickshank who was also a famous caricaturist.

One wonders whether Charles and Amelia actually ever met face to face between 1864 and 1892 when she lived at the Larches? No one has been able to confirm or deny this possibility to date.

Dickens died in 1870.

AMELIA EDWARDS – PHOTO COURTESY OF THE EGYPT EXPLORATION SOCIETY

Amelia moved to the Larches, Eastfield from London with her friend Ellen Braysher in 1864 after her parents died within a fortnight of each other in 1860. It was Amelia's home in Bristol for nearly 30 years.

ENTRANCE TO THE LARCHES

Amelia's house subsequently received a direct hit in the Bristol Blitz in the 1940s, but the name of the property can still be clearly seen on the righthand post.

It appears that Cruickshank, who illustrated for Charles Dickens, called at the Edwards' home in London after he had come into possession of some of Amelia's drawings. He was amazed to find that Amelia had drawn them then in 1843 and that she was only 12 years old. He asked her parents if he could take her on as a pupil, but her parents declined the invitation as they did not consider that such training would provide a suitable career path for Amelia.

However subsequently, as a writer Amelia became one of a select band of authors invited by Charles Dickens to contribute ghost stories for his magazine All the Year Round which he founded in 1859 and edited until his death in 1870. Amelia is acknowledged as one of the best Victorian ghost story writers of the Victorian era.

"Mugby Junction" (information courtesy of Wikipedia) is a set of short stories written in 1866 by Charles Dickens and collaborators, Charles Collins, Amelia Edwards, Andrew Halliday, and Hesba Stretton. It was first published in a Christmas edition of the magazine All the Year Round. Dickens penned a majority of the issue, including the frame narrative in which "the Gentleman for Nowhere," who has spent his life cloistered in the firm Barbox Brothers & Co., makes use of his new-found freedom in retirement to explore the rail lines that connect with Mugby Junction. Dickens's collaborators each contributed an individual story to the collection.

Amelia produced some of the Victorian era's best ghost stories including The Phantom Coach which was first published in 1864 as well as The North Mail, The New Pass and Monsieur Maurice.

Ghost stories by Charles Dickens include: To Be Taken with a Grain of Salt, No. 1

By the 1880s Amelia Edwards had also achieved global fame as an Egyptologist, travelling to the USA and other countries to give lectures as well.

Amelia sadly died in a nursing home in Weston super Mare in 1892.

∧∧∧∧∧∧∧∧∧∧∧∧∧∧∧∧∧∧∧∧∧∧∧∧∧∧∧∧∧∧∧∧∧∧

2006 – Bristol & Clifton Dickens Society on safari

BRISTOL & CLIFTON DICKENS SOCIETY MEMBERS – PHOTO FROM THE SYLVIA KELLY COLLECTION

In 2006, members of the Bristol & Clifton Dickens Society were invited by Sylvia Kelly to join this Henleaze local residents' event.

Sylvia Kelly, who joined The Henleaze Society in its first year in 1973, was also a member of many other organisations, including the Bristol & Clifton Dickens Society.

http://www.dickens-society.org.uk/B&CDS/Welcome.html

Using Claremont School as a base in May 2006, Sylvia arranged the Henleaze Safari to follow the highest points in the area which included an impromptu visit to the Briars, formerly Henleaze Farm, thanks to the kindness of its owners who were relaxing in the garden on the lovely sunny afternoon. The walkers had been viewing the old horse mounting block in adjacent Kenton Mews and had subsequently been admiring this nearby historic property from the end of the drive.

TAKING TEA AT CLAREMONT

The Safari event finished back in Claremont with cakes and a very welcome cup of tea. Members from the Bristol & Clifton Dickens Society can be seen relaxing. The Safari was jointly led by local residents Sylvia Kelly and Veronica Bowerman.

∧∧∧∧∧∧∧∧∧∧∧∧∧∧∧∧∧∧∧∧∧∧∧∧∧∧∧∧∧

AN ELOPEMENT REVEALED BY A FAMILY MEMBER 90 YEARS LATER

Rosemary Edwards' (nee Huxtable) grandmother, Mrs Edith Bruce Cole was known as 'Gaggy' by her grandchildren. Edith, the widow of Caleb Bruce Cole, lived in Claremont House (now Claremont School) until the 1940s. Rosemary recalled that 'Gaggy' was always dressed in a black full-length outfit with a black hat. Her grandfather, Caleb, a Bristol chocolate entrepreneur, died in 1912. Mrs Bruce Cole's chauffeur, who drove a Buick was called Mr Baker. The double garage which housed the car has, in recent years, been turned into a private dwelling.

Rosemary Huxtable's mother, Joyce Bruce Cole was the second

eldest of five children. Her elder brother was Brian and her other siblings were Geoffrey, Roger and Barbara. The latter died when she was 21 years old.

Joyce and Lesley Huxtable met soon after he was demobilised from the Gloucestershire regiment after the First World War. It appears that 'Gaggy' (Rosemary's grandmother and Joyce's mother) did not approve of Joyce's suitor, probably because he had neither money nor profession. However, Joyce and Lesley were in love and the only alternative to them was a runaway marriage. This was achieved by Lesley placing a ladder under Joyce's bedroom window one night and silently stealing away (c1920-1921).

The marriage of Joyce and Lesley was a success and they produced two boys and three girls. The five children in age order were David, Pat, Ann, Rosemary and Cherry. Sadly, all Rosemary's siblings have died. Although Rosemary is now 85 years-old she enjoys working as a volunteer in a local charity shop in Hampshire.

More details about the Bruce Coles and Claremont can be found in Henleaze Connections.

The dining room in Claremont House seated 20. Derek Reynolds who recalled his memories of 'Gaggy' in the second edition of The Henleaze Book was a cousin on Rosemary's father's side and used to live in Cornwall before WWII.

***1937 – THE HUXTABLES AND SOME OF THEIR COUSINS ON HOLIDAY
IN CORNWALL***

(L-R) Rosemary, Felicity, Ann, Rosemary, Audrey, Pat, David, Jane and Cherry. The five children underlined were Huxtables, the others were their cousins.

The Huxtable family initially lived at the Round House at Hemel Hempstead; then at Pallingham Quay, Sussex before settling into an isolated farm with 60 acres about three miles from Pulborough near Toat Monument. Lesley grew six apple orchards of 10 acres each from scratch. Rosemary recalls the children flying their kites from this monument about a mile away from their home. The six-sided brick tower - approximately 200 feet above sea level - was built in memory of John Drinkwater in 1827 by one of his three sons Samuel, to view the local hunting.

JOYCE HUXTABLE (NEE BRUCE COLE) AND LESLEY HUXTABLE

The Huxtables enjoying their Sussex garden in 1951.

Further details about the Bruce Cole family can be found in The Henleaze Book and also Henleaze Connections.

For more information on these publications see:

https://www.amazon.co.uk/Veronica-Bowerman/e/B001JS6O7U

Many thanks to Rosemary Edwards (nee Huxtable) for divulging this part of Henleaze's social history and also for providing the above historic photos from her family's archives. This story also appeared in the January 2018 edition of the free monthly Henleaze Book Newsletter.

∧∧∧∧∧∧∧∧∧∧∧∧∧∧∧∧∧∧∧∧∧∧∧∧∧∧∧∧

GEORGE PALMER

'My grandfather George Henry Palmer was a WW1 Royal Flying Corps (RFC) pilot during WW1.'

'He was born on 29th Oct 1897 and died 30th Oct 1985. He married Edna Ward Pike who was born in 1900 and they were married at St Mary Magdalene, Stoke Bishop, Bristol on 23rd May 1923. They initially lived in Park Grove, Henleaze before moving to 25 Lawrence Grove in the early 1930s. Edna, my grandmother died in 1969 but my grandfather continued to live in Lawrence Grove on his own until 1985 when he moved to New Cote. (In the 1960s New Cote, a home to provide additional residential care to older people, was built next to Cote House, Westbury on Trym).

'The Military Record date is 1916 for George Henry Palmer showing him as a member of the 27th RFC squadron. As a second lieutenant he completed his training at Oxford, but he was later promoted to Flight Officer. The 27th squadron flew Martinsyde G100 Elephant extensively throughout the Great War.'

GEORGE PALMER – WITH A MARTINSYDE G100 ELEPHANT

Nigel Palmer was left his Grandfather's two medals awarded at the end of the Great War: the British War Medal known as 'Squeak' shown on the left and also the Allied Victory Medal known as 'Wilfred' on the right, plus his MBE awarded in 1956 for his services to the Gas Industry.

WW1 MEDALS

These were awarded to officers and men of the British and Imperial Forces who either entered a theatre of war or entered service overseas between 5 August 1914, and 11 November 1918 inclusive. The recipient's service number, rank, name and unit were impressed on the rim.

THE 27TH SQUADRON BADGE

The squadron is still in operation and based in Odiham, Hants. Their badge, which depicts an elephant was approved by HM King Edward VIII in October 1936.

It commemorates the squadron's first operational aircraft - the Martinsyde G100 'Elephant' flown in the Great War - and also the unit's long sojourn to India. When Nigel's grandfather came home from the First World War, he trained to be a chartered accountant with a firm based in Whiteladies Road, Bristol near where the BBC now stands. The South West Gas Board were one of their customers. They were so impressed with Grandfather's work that they offered him a job. As the they were based in Bath, they arranged for him to be chauffeur driven there and back. He had endured several crashes during the First World War and these bad experiences put him off learning to drive a car. By the time he retired from the South West Gas Board he was their Treasurer and Head Accountant. The MBE awarded for his services to the gas industry was posted on 6 Jan 1956 and he received it 6th Mar 1956.

'My Aunt Joan, (my father's older sister) was born 15th June 1926 which was also my mother's date of birth. My father was born 24th Jan 1928. Joan died 24th Dec 1959, my father on 20th Mar 2002 and mother in 2004. My father was Canon Derek Palmer. My father and mother worshipped in St Peter's, Henleaze with Aunt Joan. My grandfather's sister, Kitty's family still lives in Bristol, but I am not sure where and my dad's cousin, Margaret still lives in Westbury on Trym. Dad remembers visiting my grandfather's parents who lived in Oak Lodge, Stoke Bishop (a grade II listed building on Stoke Hill).'

Acknowledgements: My thanks to: Nigel Palmer, grandson of George Henry Palmer, Matt Smith at the RAF Benevolent Fund and the following websites for providing information about George Palmer relating to his life, time as a World War One pilot and his subsequent career with the South West Gas Board.

Much Love – the online Tribute charity:

https://george-henry-palmer.muchloved.com/

Virtual Aircraft Museum:

http://www.aviastar.org/air/england/martinsyde_g-100.php

The Martinsyde File by Ray Sanger:

https://www.amazon.co.uk/Martinsyde-File-Ray-Sanger/dp/0851302734

Royal Air Force Benevolent Fund:

https://www.rafbf.org/about-us/our-organisation

Surrey in the Great War: a county remembers:

http://www.surreyinthegreatwar.org.uk/story/elephants-and-buzzards-the-contribution-of-martinsyde-aeroplanes-to-the-war-in-the-air/

∧∧∧∧∧∧∧∧∧∧∧∧∧∧∧∧∧∧∧∧∧∧∧∧∧∧∧∧∧∧

THE WEST CROFT PONIES

Memories and photos courtesy of Barbara (nee Pettit), former Henleaze resident.

'After reading about Waterdale House in a previous Henleaze Book newsletter it set me thinking about the days when my family lived in West Croft, Henleaze.

'I went to Henleaze primary schools from 1953 until 1960 and my family lived in Henleaze until 1973 when my father moved away. I used to swim at the Blind School and then Henleaze Lake and I got married in Henleaze Congregational Church, but have not lived in Henleaze (or Bristol) for many years now.

49

7 AND 8 WEST CROFT HENLEAZE, ARE IN THE BACKGROUND. PHOTO C1957/59

Three of the residents in in this small cul de sac owned a pony, during the 1950s and 1960s.

WEST CROFT - JANUARY, 1963

'I took the photographs standing outside my friend's house in Cransley Crescent, also ex Henleaze Junior School. We were going to Henbury Golf Course with the toboggan – as we did almost every day that winter. Schools were mostly closed so we had lots of time spare to make the most of it.

'Looking again at the photos, it just never occurred to us that it was so slippery that probably many older people couldn't get out to do any shopping, not that the shops had much to buy in the early part of that winter, we were far too busy enjoying ourselves and earning pocket money pushing cars up Falcondale Road!

'My childhood in Henleaze during the 1950s revolved around swimming, horses and drawing.

'We used to swim firstly at the open-air pool at the Blind School, as we called it, and when we had to go from there (it was age related) on to Henleaze Lake. As to the swimming side, I was a member of the Blind School swimming club until you had to leave (I think by the time you were 13 or so) and joined Henleaze Lake, you had to take a test to see if you could swim well enough to join, I believe this is still the case. There was a sort of pontoon in the lake then that you swam to and back again for the test. About five years ago I met up with my old neighbour's older sister, who was a friend of my older cousin who at that time lived in Cransley Crescent, to have a trip down memory lane at the Lake. They very kindly showed us around, the changing rooms smelt just as they always had done – but the sand pit had moved! I remember that particularly well as when my poor cousin got landed with taking me with her, she played for Henleaze Lake's water polo side and was an excellent swimmer having represented England, I used to sit and play in the sand pit!

'My greatest ambition was to own a pony of my own. Luckily, the first shop on Wellington Hill West was the post office where Mrs Childs worked, she helped me, a horse-mad child, with my post office account saving up for my pony; next shop along there was

Mr Curtis who had the grocery shop and used to let us have broken biscuits; next along was Aris the greengrocer, the shop was then run by the two daughters Gay and then Pat Aris. I think Pat is in one of the class photos on the **https://www.facebook.com/henleazebook/** link. Then there was Newman's the hardware shop that always had a tea chest of hardboard offcuts for sale outside. (I used to buy these offcuts for a few pennies and turn them into fields, with the help of plaster of Paris, matchsticks, electric wire and chicken wire, and old shoe boxes into a toy farm, I sold it eventually to a teacher who was going to teach in India to show her pupils what an English farm looked like. This went into my pony fund!) Then there was the off licence that had a really interesting till that used to fascinate me as a child, (we used to collect and take back all the empty bottles for the few pence we got for returning them), then there was the hairdresser. We used all these shops on a regular basis as it was pre-supermarkets then, I expect they've all gone or at least changed now.'

EDITOR'S NOTE: Sadly, they have all changed owners. Can one of our readers let us have an up to date list of the shops here or any further information on the above please?

'My first place of interest was Eastfield School of Equitation run then by Miss Joan Tripp, this was in Eastfield, which ran from Eastfield Road through to Henleaze Road. The stables were on the left-hand side as you went from Eastfield Road to Henleaze Road, I believe an estate of bungalows now marks the spot. The premises consisted of a yard of about 14 boxes, an outdoor arena and a small grazing area. The ponies were grazed mid-week at Cherry Orchards, Westbury on Trym. Miss Tripp later married and became known to us as Mrs Waddy Warr and moved to Rudgeway and ran a stud. Waddy then either sold or rented Eastfield to Mr and Mrs Brunner, I can't remember when this closed down for good and was developed.

'After saving for many years I finally reached my goal of owning my own pony. Pat Aris, and her sister, Gay from the shops nearby in Wellington Hill West were also horsey and ex HJS pupils. Pat very kindly lent me her saddle until I could afford one myself.'

'I was very lucky with our neighbours in those days as our neighbour next door kept a pony and another was an art teacher who kept a horse. Having three horse owners in a road of eight houses probably was a bit unusual!'

'I left Henleaze Junior School in 1959/1960 but, for a few years, we used to return to give pony rides there on their open days, and also at St Ursula's, which was great fun with the added bonus of lovely strawberry teas! Our takings went into their fund-raising efforts. You probably wouldn't dare to do that these days without a full suit of armour and several million pounds worth of public liability Insurance!

'I wonder if any of the children from Henleaze Junior School or St Ursula's schools remember us giving the rides?'

'We then moved our ponies out to the then quiet country lane called Passage Road - that morphed into Cribbs Causeway. We used to ride home through Badock's Wood and regularly rode over Clifton Suspension Bridge to ride in Ashton Court.'

'I don't know where I got my horse obsession from, my father wasn't the remotest bit interested and my mother was frightened of them. However, the love of horses stayed with me all my life and I always kept them, my last one died six years ago and I decided it was time to call a halt to it after so many years of horse keeping.'

'Judy Lane and I used to give pony rides at Henleaze Junior School and also at St Ursula's during their annual fetes. My grey pony was called Misty. (Judy was a lifelong friend and neighbour who sadly died in January, 2018).

'Our ponies were kept briefly in the grounds of Waterdale House, and on a smallholding opposite the back entrance to Claremont House, formerly known as Henleaze Park Farm, then The Briars and now 7 Kenton Mews.'

EDITOR'S NOTE: Six new properties were built along the lane to the latter which was at the end of a cul de sac in 1976. This lane then became a wider road with tarmac and was given the name Kenton Mews.

∧∧∧∧∧∧∧∧∧∧∧∧∧∧∧∧∧∧∧∧∧∧∧∧∧∧∧∧∧∧∧∧∧

THE RESIDENT WITH A BOATING LAKE IN HER GARDEN

In the 1990s Natalie Griffey gave her 1927 Henleaze Swimming Club membership card, registered 234, to Veronica Bowerman, compiler of The Henleaze Book.

The Club has subsequently been given this membership card for their archives.

In the 1960s Natalie Griffey lived with her family at Waterdale House which was demolished during this decade and replaced by the Fire Station on Southmead Road. In the grounds of Waterdale which was bordered by Wellington Hill West and Southmead Road there was a lake. In the summer it was used by the family and the local community for boating and in the winter, when cold enough, for skating. The lake is behind the wall on Wellington Hill West. Waterdale House can just be seen in the background. Photo from the Griffey collection. A fire was lit in the mock Adam fireplace in the hut in the centre of the picture to keep skaters warm in the winter. The hut was also used by the bathers in summer for changing purposes and as storage for the boat.

C1960S WATERDALE LAKE

The lake was drained in the 1960s and Waterdale Gardens and Close built on the land there. Photo courtesy of the Griffey family.

More details about Waterdale House and Henleaze Swimming Club can be found in **https://www.amazon.co.uk/Henleaze-Book-Veronica-Bowerman/dp/0955356709**

∧∧∧∧∧∧∧∧∧∧∧∧∧∧∧∧∧∧∧∧∧∧∧∧∧∧∧∧∧∧∧

JOHN WHITE ROBISON - HEAD MASTER AND BOWLS CHAMPION EXTRAORDINAIRE

JOHN WHITE ROBISON CIRCA 1940

Photo courtesy of researchers Liz and Murray Cameron.

'An interesting personality moved into the Golden Hill area following his retirement in 1933 as a Head Master. From his newly built home at 22 Stadium Road, he launched himself into a second career as a sportsman; finally becoming a National Bowls Champion!

'John was a Scotsman, born in 1873 in Lochmaben, Dumfriesshire a small town some 25-30 miles north west of Carlisle, close to Lockerbie, scene of the Pan Am flight bombing of 1988.

'John's mother Ann died whilst he was an infant and his father Robert married again to Jane Hyslop in 1875. The family finally comprised of nine known children and John lived with his grandparents to ease the strain on accommodation.

'In due course John entered the teaching profession, moved south and spent many years specialising in the teaching of deaf children in the Liverpool area. It was here that he met and married his first wife Florence Walker in 1905, a Yorkshire lass who was an assistant school mistress, and a teacher of deaf children; they were both 32 years old. They were married at a Congregational Church in Florence's home town of Leeds.

'John continued honing his professional skills as a teacher and some four years later in 1909 the couple's first child arrived, a little girl; Margaret Lowe Robison. The family continued through the World War One years and in 1918 a great opportunity opened up for John. He was appointed Head Master of a Bristol school for deaf children and he and his family duly took up residence in the school at Kingsdown.

'The Bristol Kingsdown Institution for Deaf Children was the first state-funded residential school in Bristol; all previous boarding schools for the deaf had been privately run institutions. The building which originally housed Kingsdown High School for Girls, established in 1868 and also known as Marlborough House Girls School became the Kingsdown School in 1898. Although capable of taking 42 boarding pupils, the Education Department restricted the school to just 31.

'The first Head Master of Kingsdown was Octavius Illingworth and with his wife serving as Matron, he remained in charge for 20 years. So far as teaching the deaf was concerned Illingworth was a pure oralist, but in1900 permission was granted to the school to run classes in manual methods for those pupils for whom the oral system was not appropriate.

'However, a serious shock awaited John; no sooner had he settled the family in, his wife Florence passed away at the early age of 45 years; their young daughter Margaret was just 9 years old. Florence had succumbed to the 1918 flu pandemic which turned out be one of the deadliest natural disasters in human history. Typically, the onset was devastatingly quick. Those fine and healthy at breakfast could be dead by tea-time. Within hours of feeling the first symptoms of fatigue and headache some victims would rapidly develop pneumonia and start turning blue, signalling a shortage of oxygen. They would then struggle for air until they suffocated to death. More people died of influenza in that single year than in the four years of the Black Death Bubonic Plague.

'John's mind must surely have moved from the exuberance of his new position to one of complete devastation.

'John remained in residence as Head Master for some 15 years, retiring at 60 years of age in 1933, at which point the school was closed down and the day pupils transferred to Moorfields Deaf Council School near Lawrence Hill Station and many of the boarding pupils were sent to other towns and cities to continue their education.

'It was now all happening for John; this same year he married Lily Faux, a teacher he had known for some years. John and Lily were 60 and 48 years of age respectively.

'This was a new beginning for John having been a widower for some 15 years and he and Lily set up home together in a newly completed house at 22 Stadium Road, in the Golden Hill area.

'John now developed a keen interest in the game of bowls and in due course joined the local Henleaze Bowling Club.

'Meanwhile, in 1936 John's daughter Margaret, 27 years old, married a young man from Coombe Dingle – George Leigh, at Westbury Parish Church. The bride had lived with her father in Stadium Road until then.

'Henleaze Bowling Club was founded in 1928 when Clarence Davey purchased land opposite his house in Grange Court Road and with some friends, set about forming a bowling club. The club was incorporated on the 14 June 1928.

'John was soon showing a natural aptitude for bowling and was a member of Gloucestershire's Middleton Cup winning team of

1936.

Other successes followed: Bath Open Pairs in 1937

Gloucestershire County Pairs in 1939

Weston Open Pairs and CCBBA Pairs & Rinks in 1940

'In 1945 he was runner-up in the EBA singles. He was also Captain of Gloucestershire, runner up in the GBA singles and skipped the rink that won the GBA Fours. John also went on to win the CCBA pairs again in 1950 at the age of 77 years!

'In 1946 'Robbie' as he was known to club members was awarded his International 'Cap', a wonderful honour for himself and for the club.

'John passed away in June 1960 suffering from heart disease at his home in Golden Hill with his wife Lily present. Lily died two years later in a nursing home in Clevedon from bronchopneumonia; They were 87 and 77 years old respectively.

'John bequeathed his home at 22 Stadium Road to his wife Lily, together with all contents including the large collection of bowling trophies that he had accumulated. He did however exclude his prized set of 'Henselite' bowls which he bequeathed to his old friend Harry Markell.'

∧∧∧∧∧∧∧∧∧∧∧∧∧∧∧∧∧∧∧∧∧∧∧∧∧∧∧∧∧∧∧∧∧∧

SIDNEY CURTIS

Introduction

COMPILER'S NOTE: When I compiled the second edition of The Henleaze Book in the early 1990s, I kept coming across the name Sidney Curtis - mainly relating to the Henleaze Park estate and

Henleaze Lake. I quickly realised that from the late 1910s until the 1940s the services that he and his sons offered were really important to the development of Henleaze.

Until I researched information for St Margaret's: Memories, Musings & Merriment I was unable to find anyone that could give me any further information about Sidney. Fortunately, his eldest granddaughter, Shirley Chapman (nee Curtis), an 'old gel' of St Margaret's, was able to help. She told me that she was one of Sidney' five grandchildren and that her youngest brother, Chris, had paperwork relating to their grandfather which could enable me to obtain a more detailed view of his life.

So, with Chris' help, I have now been able to highlight the many diverse and interesting projects in Henleaze in which entrepreneur Sidney had been involved.

These included: leaseholder for swimming at Henleaze Lake, owner of the business S Curtis & Sons Builders with premises at the junction of Henleaze and Eastfield Roads, (subsequently owned by the Clark family from 1927) owner of the Mortar Mills on the junction of Eastfield and Southmead Roads (across the road from Amelia Lodge) and office premises at Westbury Hill, Holmes Grove and Henleaze Road. The family had lived at Springfield Farm (Springfield Cottages) from as early as 1914 and worked as farmers there – highlighted by farm items for sale advertisements included in the Western Daily Press from that year until 1923. It is thought that Sidney started S Curtis & Sons during the latter year when he had the opportunity to purchase the Springfield Farm Estate land where he created and sold 19 tennis courts in what is now the extended area of Russell Grove. This additional income also helped Sidney Curtis, when living at Springfield Farm, to purchase Henleaze Park Estate with the house and its remaining parcels of land for £20,500 during that same year. The purchase of Glenwood Estates and Southmead Manor followed. From the mid-1910s until the mid-1930s, as well as buying land and building houses, S Curtis & Sons organised surveys, marketed and sold properties, constructed tennis courts and built many new roads in the area, including those adjacent to St Peter's Church.

Many thanks also to Bristol Archives, St Peter's Church, Henleaze Tennis Club, Westbury Tennis Club and Henleaze Swimming Club for their assistance.

Veronica Bowerman

Family Background

Sidney Curtis was born 5 or 6 May, 1879 at Old Down, near Rudgeway.

His father Mark Curtis was born in 1833 and his mother Emma Curtis (nee Fream) in 1838. In the 1861 census Mark and Emma were married but living at home with William and Sarah, Mark's parents at Olveston. Both William and Mark are described as "Ag Labs" - agricultural labourers.

At the time of the 1891 census Mark and Emma had a home of their own and a growing family. Mark's occupation was given then as an 'employee working on his own'. They lived in Schumac Cottage, Old Down which was built on the lines of a Swiss cottage. Sidney was one of their nine children shown in this photo taken outside the cottage.

***C1889/90 - THE CURTIS FAMILY AT OLD DOWN. SIDNEY, THE
YOUNGEST IS SITTING CROSS-LEGGED***

Sid married Flo on 26 May 1901 at St Michael and All Angels,
Pigsty Hill, Gloucester Road. (Sadly, in.1990 it was declared
structurally unsound. There was much protest but it was closed in
1991 and demolished 1997). Sid died at Southmead Hospital on
26 or 27 July 1954 aged 75.

C1897-99 SIDNEY CURTIS

1901 - FLORENCE MINNIE CURTIS (NEE CREW) AGED 18

Florence Minnie Crew was born on 23 September 1882 and married Sidney on 26 May 1901. Flo died on 16 January 1971 at 193 Wellington Hill West aged 87.

On their marriage, in 1901 Sid and Flo lived in the property now known as 97 Coombe Lane, near the junction of Dingle Road. Both their sons were born there in 1902 and 1904. Later, as S Curtis & Sons, their building business grew and they kept moving to be on hand at the many projects that ensued in the Henleaze area.

Children

Sidney and Flo had two children.

Lewis Granville was born in 1902 and died in 1968. He was married to Maisie, nee Banfield, at St John's church, Clifton on 6 December 1928. They had no children.

Graham Henry was born on 16 February 1904 and died on 20 Nov 1975. He married Violet, nee Cox in August 1928.

Both sons worked in the family business, S Curtis & Sons, assisting in a wide range of surveying, building and marketing projects.

Grandchildren

Sidney and Flo had five grandchildren.

Ainslie, the eldest had married into the Saunders' family and lived in the cottage behind their house and business on 223 Henleaze Road. The business was known as F E Saunders Ltd, painting and decorating contractors. The couple emigrated to Canada but returned home and divorced. In order to obtain enough money to pay for their fare to Canada. Ainslie also worked at nearby Roper's Dairy, on the other side of Henleaze Road, starting at

5am each morning delivering milk to Henleaze residents before starting his main work. Ainslie sadly died on 29 March, 2006.

Shirley, Deidre, Lawrence and Chris are the four younger grandchildren.

Sidney Curtis' work and projects

Sidney initially worked for himself as a greengrocer in Easton Road and later as a butcher in Westbury Park – near the Etloe and Berkeley Roads junction where he appears to have bought the property. The names of these two shops are unknown to his family and also when Sidney started working at either shop, although it could possibly have been during the 1890s at Easton.

Around 1911 - Dr Badock rented the lake from Henry Green and stocked it for fishing Also, from about 1912, he leased part of it to a third party (Sidney Curtis) who admitted the public for bathing.

'From about 1912 - a Mr Curtis charged people to swim at the lake, which became known as the Westbury bathing place or Henleaze bathing pool. It was very popular, with up to 200 people in the water on sunny days, and the whole length of the lake was used for swimming.' See this link for more details:

http://www.henleazeswimmingclub.org/about-us/the-story-of-the-lake/

He appointed a superintendent, Mr Voysey to help. Swimming was a great success in the summer and also skating in the winter when the lake froze over.

Chris Curtis, Sidney's youngest grandson recalls being told that his grandmother, Flo Curtis (during the mid-1910s) when the lake was frozen over, cooked hot meals for the skaters to enjoy using bonfires she organised for such events.

C LATE 1910s - SKATERS, INCLUDING SOLDIERS ON THE ICE AT HENLEAZE LAKE

1913, July - Henleaze Park Estate did not reach the reserve price of £10,000 at the auction. So, after a group of interested parties F. N Cowlin, the builders and also the agents, Wansbrough, the solicitors and Horace Walker, Chairman of H J Packer & Co Ltd, chocolate manufacturers were able to purchase the estate for £8,750. With the help of local resident Sidney Curtis parcels of land were laid out in the area around Wanscow Walk, Henleaze Park Drive, Park Grove, Oakwood Road and Hill View and subsequently developed for housing.

The landowners bordering the Henleaze Park House estate at that time were:

Trustees of the late C Bruce Cole Esq, The British Land Co Ltd, Representatives of the late Rev G E Whitbourne, F S Green Esq and Sir J Weston-Stevens.

The original borders now roughly follow the roads that were subsequently built: The Drive, Henleaze Park, left at the end between the back gardens of Kenton Mews and Golden Hill playing fields, behind Henleaze Park Farm to the top of Henleaze Park Drive, across to Walliscote Road, then left into the Crescent to the Hill View junction, down Rockside Drive, left into Henleaze Road, back to junction at the Drive.

By 1914 - Sidney and Flo Curtis and their young sons were living at what was then known as Springfield Farm (now known as Springfield Cottages situated in Russell Grove). This is confirmed by various items for sale by Sidney advertised in the Western Dail/y Press.

1915-1917 - at the turn of the 18th century limestone was quarried in the Southmead area. It was a general practice for the local landowners to lease out such quarries; an example of this practice were the Llewellins, owners of the quarry now known as Henleaze Lake. Richard 111 Lewellin remained a bachelor until he died in 1871.The joint estates (Holmwood House and Southmead Manor) were then bought and owned by Henry Green from 1872 to 1924.

Quarrying ceased production after 1903 and the quarry was allowed to fill with water. The quarry was also known as Southmead, Shellards and subsequently Henleaze Lake.

According to Henleaze Swimming Club, a Mr Weeks of Henleaze Road was charging people to swim at the Lake from at least 1910.There was swimming before this as other press reports confirm.

March, 1916 - the Springfield House Estate had been owned by Lieut. Col Cecil Francis Heyworth Savage for several years but to legalise his possession in March 1916, solicitor Jeremiah Clarke swore a statutory declaration to confirm his title. It was assumed that there were no formal deeds of the property extant at that time. It had been decided to change the use of Springfield House, a private dwelling, to Northumberland House School for Girls in 1912. The declaration had also been necessary in order to dispose of some of the land from the estate - 11 acres (4.5 hectares) of the estate to the east of Henleaze Road. Florence Curtis, wife of Sidney took out a yearly tenancy agreement that month with the Lieut. Col for land and cottages at Springfield. Her guarantor was her mother, Mrs Elizabeth Crew.

1916 - 1917 - it is probable that the main leaseholder, Stanley Badock, put a stop to swimming at Henleaze Lake because of two drownings during these years.

1919 - following these drownings in Henleaze Lake a group of swimmers led by Albert Wain, who had been enjoying swimming in the lake for some time, proposed establishing a club under strict Amateur Swimming Association rules so that swimming could be resumed and managed in this way.

After an energetic campaign, Henleaze Swimming Club was formed and took over the management of the lake in May, 1919.

From 1919-1923 - the main leaseholder, Stanley Badock sublet the Lake to the Henleaze Swimming Club.

1922, 23 August - Cecil Francis Heyworth-Savage sold the renamed Springfield Building Estate to Sidney Curtis.

GRADONIT, HENLEAZE PARK DRIVE

1922 - the garden pictured here was laid out when the property was built on part of the former Henleaze Park Estate by Sidney Curtis & Sons. The company often landscaped the gardens of new builds before selling. We have been unable to pinpoint the exact location of this house, to date. Can you help?

1923 – Henleaze Park Estate - the house and its remaining parcels of land were sold to Sidney Curtis of Springfield Farm for £20,500. It is believed that the Curtis family lived in Henleaze Park House for that year until it was sold again in 1924 to a local school.

An excerpt from Elizabeth's Ralph's book – A Short History of St Peter's Henleaze – 'When in 1923 the Henleaze Park Estate was laid out as a building site, it was thought that a church on this estate would be more centrally placed for the great majority of people living in this area. And so, a plot land, just over one acre,

(0.4 hectares) was purchased for £1,427. (Just over £77,000 in 2017's money) from S Curtis & Sons.' Sidney asked the Bristol Diocesan Board to donate a small part of the road cost for access roads similar to the ones he had already built in the area. The services and materials needed to complete the road work were then provided free of charge by S Curtis & Sons. Elizabeth Ralph was the third City Archivist for Bristol and she had lived with her family for some years in Henleaze.

1923, from March - Sidney had started developing part of the land on the Springfield Building Estate in the Russell Grove area as tennis courts.

Plots 14, 15, 16 and 17 then known as the David Thomas Memorial Lawn Tennis Club were leased for a rent of £32 per annum.

Sidney sold plots, 18 & 19 (on the left at the end of Tennessee Grove) to the elders of Henleaze Congregational Church (as it was then).

1923 – by the end of the year - four local churches had initially purchased and run tennis clubs from part of the Springfield Building Estate:

Henleaze Congregational Church (as it was then) for Henleaze Lawn Tennis Club

Plots 18 and 19

St Alban's Church for Westbury Park Tennis Club

Plots 3, 4, 5, 6, 7, 8, 9 and 10

Trinity Presbyterian (church originally in Cranbrook Road) for their tennis club

Plots 11 and 12

<u>Redland Park United Reformed Church/ Highbury Chapel for David Thomas Memorial Tennis Club</u>

Plots 14,15, 16 and 17

Highbury Chapel, founded in 1843, was a thriving and wealthy church under its patriarchal first minister, the Rev David Thomas. In 1860 the church meeting of Highbury decided that a Congregational Church was needed in the rapidly expanding Redland area. A suitable site was sought and a desirable one found on the corner of Redland Park and Whiteladies Road, a piece of land which was part of Mr Garaway's market garden, and it was purchased for £700.

1923, 10 November - it is thought that from 1913 Sidney Curtis would also have been helping the three owners of the Henleaze Park estate develop the area for housing purposes. So, when the family were still living at Springfield Farm, the opportunity to purchase Henleaze Park House and its remaining parcels of land arose and Sidney was also able to purchase Henleaze Park Estate for £20,500.

1924 - Sidney sold Henleaze Park house and land of 6.25 acres (2.5 hectares) to the Rev G A K Simpson and his wife Caroline. The house became the new premises for St Margaret's High School for Girls who were, until then, located in Downs Park West. Caroline Simpson and her sister Emily Campbell were joint heads of the school.

ST MARGARET'S SCHOOL FOR GIRLS. PHOTO COURTESY OF FORMER PUPIL, VALERIE ARVELO, NEE BONNER, C1960s

1924 - Stanley Badock then bought from Henry Green 83 acres that originally belonged to the Llewellin family which included Henleaze Lake. The latter was leased by the new owner Stanley Badock to the Henleaze Swimming Club from 1924 – 1933.

For more information see:

http://www.henleazeswimmingclub.org/about-us/the-story-of-the-lake/

May, 1925 - a strip of land was purchased by the David Thomas Memorial Lawn Tennis Club from S Curtis & Sons to give access from Tennessee Grove.

1925 - a part of the remaining Henleaze Park Estate was sold to the builder Monk Bros for £787.10s.0d (£787.50) for new builds in Henleaze Park Drive. Further parcels of land were sold off to other builders included these areas: Park Grove, Oakwood Road, etc.

Mid 1920s – the photo shows workers at the Mortar Mills in Lake Road with Graham and Lewis Curtis. The car belonged to Graham. Sidney Curtis later sold the Mortar Mills to Southmead Mortar Company.

WORKERS AT THE MORTAR MILLS, C1926, AT THE JUNCTION OF EASTFIELD AND SOUTHMEAD ROADS. GRAHAM IS CENTRE WITH HANDS IN HIS COAT POCKETS. LEWIS IS THIRD FROM THE RIGHT TOWARDS THE BACK.

The Council used to regularly bring over cinders from all parts of the City in order to ensure that the mill recycled them into mortar for building purposes. The entrance to the mills would have been approximately where 158-168 Eastfield Road now stand, opposite Amelia Lodge.

1926 – at auction, lot 1, where the Southmead Manor was located was purchased by Mr White. Lot 2 - the Glenwood and Lake Roads area was bought for development by Sidney Curtis & Sons.

Once some of the properties were built Sidney and Flo moved into and lived in Broadways, now numbered 11 Lake Road, Graham in no 8 opposite and Lewis just around the corner at 11 Glenwood Road. Tennis courts were also built by them on the land roughly where Merlin Court, an age exclusive development, is now located in Lake Road. Lot 3 - highlighted as pasture land and a suitable building site - was later developed as a police station.

1927 – Sidney Curtis & Sons remodelled Southmead Manor as two houses. The Whites moved into one of these houses, but later retired to Torquay in the 1950s.

1927, 21 May – This edition of the Western Daily Press includes an advertisement in Properties for Sale for S Curtis & Sons, House, Land and Estate Agents.

Mid 1920s - Knole Park, Almondsbury – when Sidney Curtis purchased the Manor House and the surrounding land. When some useful parts of buildings were demolished in the Henleaze area they were moved and recycled at Knole Park. Interestingly, the Packer and Fry chocolate families both lived for some years in the Manor House which was divided into two.

1927 – 1935 – numerous building projects in Knole Park and other places in the vicinity including Almondsbury and Pilning involving S Curtis & Sons appear in the Gloucestershire archives.

From 1931 – Sidney's eldest son, Lewis Curtis was operating as The Henleaze Estate Agency from 88 Henleaze Road. The initial properties he marketed and sold were ones developed by S Curtis & Sons. Lewis advertised regularly in the Western Daily Press.

1934 – at its peak S Curtis & Sons had a fleet of 12 lorries. One of the these was involved in an accident outside the Beehive, Wellington Hill West.

C1934 – ONE OF THE LORRIES FROM S CURTIS & SONS IN A HOLE BY THE BEEHIVE

Mid 1930s - land in Little Stoke, adjacent to Filton airport, was purchased for the development for 40 houses. Needless to say, from 1938 no one wanted to purchase a home by any UK airport as they had now become high priority for bombing targets by the Germans. Also, any likely prospective buyers were being drafted away from the area to assist with war efforts. So, S Curtis & Sons found themselves in a very difficult position then having invested heavily in a proposed new development with unsaleable properties.

1939, 3 September - Britain declared war on Germany and Parliament immediately passed a more wide-reaching measure. The National Service (Armed Forces) Act imposed conscription on all males aged between 18 and 41 who had to register for service.

1939-1945, during WWII – it appears that Sidney and sons Lewis and Graham were in reserved occupations during this time, probably as building repairers, to put right damage to buildings caused by bombing.

1940s - headed paper shows that the business was operating from 88 Henleaze Road - on the corner of Holmes Grove.

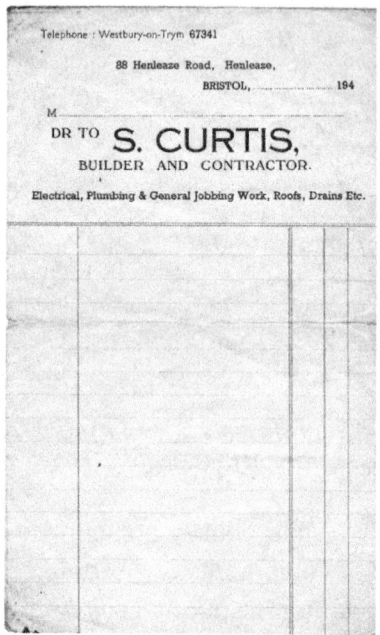

Telephone : Westbury-on-Trym 67341

88 Henleaze Road, Henleaze,

BRISTOL, ... 194

M.....................

DR TO **S. CURTIS,**
BUILDER AND CONTRACTOR.

Electrical, Plumbing & General Jobbing Work, Roofs, Drains Etc.

1940S - S CURTIS – HEADED PAPER

c1946 – Lewis, the elder son, continued as an estate agent at 88 Henleaze Road, the former business premises of S Curtis & Sons.

At that time Graham, the younger son, also set himself up in business but as a freelance estate agent.

Early 1970s – Sidney's youngest grandson Chris was taken on a nostalgic drive around Henleaze by his father, Graham, who was able to show him many of the properties that the family business S Curtis & Sons built in Henleaze during the 1920s and 1930s. Chris Curtis had taken his camera with him for the drive so he was able to photograph a selection of these properties.

2018 – spotted in Henleaze Park Drive by local historian Julian Lea-Jones, a personalised sewage cover thought to have been laid by builders, S Curtis & Sons from the early 1920s.

PHOTO 2018 – COURTESY OF JULIAN LEA JONES

Retirement

Sid retired during the late 1930s/early 1940s. Sid and Flo subsequently moved to 126 Redland Road, Bristol.

Granddaughter Shirley recalled that Sidney really enjoyed his later years with his grandchildren. He was a kind and fun-loving grandfather to them.

Additional information

The business known as S Curtis & Sons was run by Sidney and his sons Lewis and Graham. The year it started is unclear but it is thought to be by the early 1920s.

The Curtis family liked to be convenient to their work so often lived in the immediate area during their building work which included properties in Halsbury Road, Devonshire Road, Henleaze Park, Springfield Cottages, Holmes Grove and Lake Road. On quite a few occasions various members of the family would landscape the gardens of their new builds in readiness for the buyers.

Their business premises operated from the junction of Eastfield and Henleaze Roads. These were subsequently purchased by the Clark family in 1927.

Office premises were located at Holmes Grove, Henleaze Road and also probably Westbury Hill.

It is known that Sidney Curtis included some drain covers with the business details in some grounds of the houses built by his company. Local Historian, Julian Lea-Jones has been able to locate this sewage cover which would have been laid c1920 near the Henleaze Road end of Henleaze Park Drive, as can be seen from the photo he kindly took.

Please let us know if you know of any of the locations of these covers in the area, either bearing the initials SC or S Curtis & Sons, Henleaze.

Sid and Flo were living across the road from 88 Henleaze Road at 2 Holmes Grove, Sid having retired. Later they moved to Redland. Sid died in 1954 in Southmead Hospital and Flo in 1971 at 193 Wellington Hill West.

^^

THATCHING NEWS

For many people this property – the thatched cottage at 166 Henleaze Road on the junction of Wanscow Walk epitomises Henleaze.

NOVEMBER, 2017 - PHOTO COURTESY OF ELIZABETH LOEFFLER

Previous re-thatchings

1970 – PHOTO COURTESY OF THE BRISTOL POST

1994 – PHOTO FROM THE SYLVIA KELLY COLLECTION

2017 – NEW THATCH – PHOTO COURTESY OF DUNCAN OGILVIE

This property made headline news in Henleaze in 2017! This latest thatching has restored the exterior of the cottage to its former glory.

More details on the history of the house can be found in https://sites.google.com/site/henleazebook/

The property served as the Manse for the United Reformed Church based in in nearby Waterford Road in the 1920s. More details can be found in https://www.amazon.co.uk/HENLEAZE-CONNECTIONS-Some-Fascinating-Facts/dp/1520620071/ref=asap_bc?ie=UTF8

MARCH, 2018 - INTERVIEW WITH DUNCAN OGILVIE

QUESTIONS BY VERONICA BOWERMAN

ANSWERS FROM DUNCAN OGILVIE, RESIDENT OF 166 HENLEAZE ROAD

VB - What year did you buy the property?

DO - I bought the cottage in 1999.

VB - Why did you buy the home?

DO - As a young boy brought up in Westbury Park, I used to visit

Henleaze regularly with my mother to go shopping. Whenever we passed the cottage she would often say "one day, when I win the pools" as it was her dream property. Unfortunately, lady luck didn't smile on her - probably because she never did the pools! Although she didn't live long enough to see me buy the cottage, when I had the opportunity to do so I jumped at the chance.

VB - How long did the re-thatch take?

DO - The thatching only took six weeks or so. What took longer was finding somebody that had the expertise to realise my dream of giving some much needed "TLC" back to the property. Fortunately, we found this with master thatcher John Harman and his team. Using traditional methods, it was a pleasure to see them exercise their craft with skill, dedication and precision to achieve such a fantastic result.

VB - What do you think the benefits of re-thatching are?

DO - Well the obvious benefit is to keep the property watertight and help retain its value. However, I'm also aware of the place that the cottage has in the hearts of the people of Henleaze so wanted to restore the property to its former glory.

VB - Now that you have had your home re-thatched have you received many compliments from passers-by/email/telephone etc?

DO - There's been a couple of "about time too" comments which I totally agree with. However, the response to the re-thatching has been overwhelming both from passers-by and in the local media.

VB - If you ever decided to sell the property would you buy another thatched cottage?

DO - Possibly. Whilst thatched cottages are a thing of beauty, they are a purchase made as much with the heart as with the head.

VB - Do you think that the locals admire your home and if so why?

DO - With its incongruous setting, the cottage is such an iconic part of the Henleaze area that it's known to everybody. I just hope therefore that the recent re-thatch will bring a smile to passers-by and remind them what a lovely part of Bristol in which we are fortunate to live.

Some of this information appeared in the March, 2018 edition of the free Henleaze Book email newsletter.

^^^^^^^^^^^^^^^^^^^^^^^^^^^^^^^^^^^^^

WESTBURY STORES

Favoured by Best Selling Henleaze Author

Dave Hellen's father, Charles Hellen ran Westbury Stores on Westbury Hill from the 1930s, opposite the Forester's Arms (now a Tesco shop). The grocery store subsequently closed in 1968.

WESTBURY STORES - PHOTO COURTESY OF DAVE HELLEN

One of Charles' customers was Henleaze best-selling author, Margaret Harrison and her widowed sister who both lived in Henleaze Gardens. (Mrs Olive Griffiths first lived in the house when she married.)

One of her books, Where I Marry given to Charles Hellen by author Margaret Harrison

WHERE I MARRY was one of the three books that Margery Harrison, pen name Margaret Harrison, gave Charles Hellen, their grocer, over the years – two of them given still have their dustjackets.

Charles' son Dave Hellen has not read any of the books and believes that his father may not have done so either! Veronica Bowerman has since read them after Dave kindly donated them to her. She was reminded of other authors like Enid Blyton from those often-innocent days of the 1950s.

∧∧∧∧∧∧∧∧∧∧∧∧∧∧∧∧∧∧∧∧∧∧∧∧∧∧∧∧∧∧∧

CHAPTER 3 – SCHOOLS AND OPEN SPACES

THE FORMER BLIND SCHOOL SITE

Blind schools in Bristol existed from the late 1700s. A purpose-built building was started in 1907 in Henleaze and was the fourth and final location for the school in Bristol. It subsequently opened in 1911 with royal in its title given by King George V. During the 1960s, thanks for rapid advances in medicine, the number of pupils diminished. Many of the existing pupils were able to attend special or mainstream schools. It was decided to put the school and its land up for public auction in 1969 for development purposes. New roads in the former grounds include Pyecroft, Broadleys Avenue etc. The area is now popularly known as the Blind School site is adjacent to the dual carriageway on Henleaze Road.

2018 - FOUND IN A HENLEAZE GARDEN

Residents on the former Blind School site frequently turn up pieces of clay pipe stems (tobacco pipes), photo courtesy of Liz Loeffler. (A 20p coin has been included to help gauge the size).

Recent excavations in the front garden of number 2 Wyecliffe Road, suggest that the driveway to the Blind School ran between numbers 2 and 3 at a slight angle to the current driveway of number 3. The kerbstones intersect with the front corner of the garden.

The former School Lodge (demolished at the same time at the Blind School in the late 1960s) was also used by the gardeners and also the pupils to sell their wares. It appears to have been opposite the large double gates to Old Quarry Park across Henleaze Road dual carriageway; the gates that are normally locked - opened when the grass cutters come.

These excavations uncovered a trench in the back garden of

number 2, which may have been a drainage ditch.

It was filled with smashed crockery and shells (mainly coarse cream-coloured earthenware bottles and flagons, and blue and white willow pattern plates, together with a large quantity of oyster shells).

Many thanks to local resident, Liz Loeffler for sharing her story and photo.

EDITOR'S NOTE: Who brought these oyster shells here and why? These shells are similar to chalk and limestone and could have been used to create mortar?

Apparently by the end of the 18th century oyster industrialisation cheapened them, making oysters one of the staples of the diet of the poor. So, any suggestions about this location for the oyster shells and also the age of the pipes shown in the photo would be appreciated.

∧∧∧∧∧∧∧∧∧∧∧∧∧∧∧∧∧∧∧∧∧∧∧∧∧∧∧∧∧∧∧∧∧∧∧∧

Who developed the Blind School site?

Recently we received an email from a Blind School site resident, Liz Loeffler asking who the builders for the Blind School site were.

Frederick Powell, the builders, were part of the Broseley group and traded under Frederick Powell but all sites were marketed under the parent company name of Broseley.

Broseley Estates via Facebook confirmed the following information:

BROSELEY HOMES LIMITED

30 Dec 1986 - 01 Oct 1990

FREDERICK POWELL & SON LIMITED

27 Mar 1968 - 30 Dec 1986

Looking at the council planning website, it appears that planning permission was sought in 1970, which fits in with the auction date included in The Henleaze Book.

BROSELEY HOMES

Attractive GEORGIAN STYLE TOWN HOUSES in "Village Green" setting at HENLEAZE PARK, BRISTOL CITY, and conveniently situated within minutes of excellent local shops, the Downs, Motorways to London, Birmingham and South-West, and City Centre.

SHOW HOUSE Open Weekends: 2.30-4.30 p.m.

FROM £15,400 FREEHOLD with FULL CENTRAL HEATING.

STANLEY, ALDER & PRICE

94a Whiteladies Road, Bristol.
Telephone Bristol 35071.

THIS ADVERTISEMENT – COURTESY OF BROSELEY HOMES - WITH INFORMATION ON THE PROPERTIES IN 1973.

JUNE 2018 -PYECROFT AVENUE

This photo was taken by the dual carriageway on Henleaze Road. Prices for properties on the former Blind School site started at £15,400 in 1973!

Many thanks to the following people who subsequently helped us obtain the information about the former Blind School site: Bernice Gollop, Denis Sloper, Eddie Foster, Broseley Estates.

∧∧∧∧∧∧∧∧∧∧∧∧∧∧∧∧∧∧∧∧∧∧∧∧∧∧∧∧∧∧∧∧∧

The Blind School connection with New Mexico, USA

Excerpts from 2017 emails sent to Henleaze Book

Subject: Information Request about Royal Workshop for the Blind

To Whom It May Concern:

The Anderson Abruzzo Albuquerque International Balloon Museum:

www.cabq.gov/balloon

in Albuquerque, New Mexico, United States is currently hosting a series of events culminating in a balloon rally for people of all abilities and special needs. As a part of the program we are displaying a gondola from our collection that was made by the Royal Workshop for the Blind in Bristol. I am writing to inquire about information on the history of this partnership with the school to create a text panel with information. Any information, images, or appropriate contact information that you might be able to provide would be greatly appreciated. Your efforts and the source of information will be appropriately credited in the museum display. We are very excited to have this piece in our collection and to highlight it for our Rise and Try Week and Ballooning for All Rally.

Emails sent by Henleaze Book:

Many thanks for your email which was of great interest.

The Blind School in Bristol moved three times and finally closed due of increased advances in medicine in 1969. There were two dedicated workshops in Bristol as well where the gondola you mention may possibly have been made. Could you give me dates and further details of the gondola - when it was built etc. and also an image so I can hopefully come up with some copy for you? I am in touch with several former pupils who may be able to provide information as well.

Ballooning is very important to Bristol as well as Albuquerque as you probably know? In fact, the first annual Balloon Fiesta was held here in 1979 and is now one of the largest in the World.

I look forward to hearing further from you.

Email sent by the Albuquerque Balloon Museum

I apologise for my delayed response. We don't know much about the gondola. It was donated by a Glen Terry of Minnesota. Attached is a copy of the tag on the basket. It has been estimated to be from circa 1981 but I can't verify that the partnership existed at that time. I have found information about the Bristol Workshops and about Cameron Balloons but not about the connections between the two.

BASKET TAG – PHOTO COURTESY OF THE ALBUQUERQUE BALLOON MUSEUM

In her research Veronica was able to find the owner of the balloon Glen Terry, who was able to supply many photos and documentation showing its history.

Glen named his first balloon Flamebuoyant. He is still ballooning with a later version 40 years later on! (During his working life he pursued the career of a professional photographer.)

He has passed his evidence of the balloon on to the Museum as well as to Veronica. He has asked that he is acknowledged as the source when any of the photos are used in written publications or on the internet.

∧∧∧∧∧∧∧∧∧∧∧∧∧∧∧∧∧∧∧∧∧∧∧∧∧∧∧∧∧∧∧∧∧

Glen Terry's story

Here is Glen Terry's story about his first balloon, the Flamebuoyant and its basket 126CB. (N# is 126CB Serial # 324 Cameron Viva 56). It was a unique balloon of ultralight weight. Glen still has the instruments.

JULY, 1979 – FLAMEBUOYANT'S MAIDEN FLIGHT

The balloon was test inflated on 21 November, 1977 and certified airworthy in December of the same year.

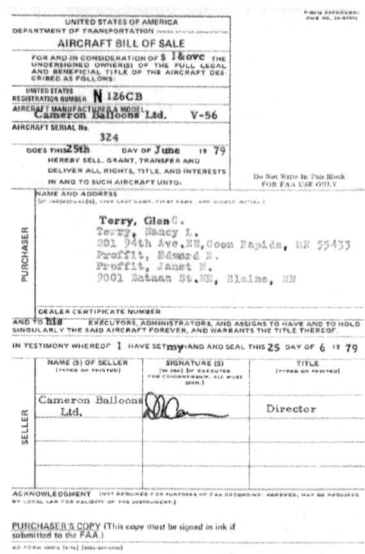

25 JUNE 1979 - AIRCRAFT BILL OF SALE

From Cameron Balloon UK:

To Glen Terry, USA: Signed by Don Cameron.

'We purchased the balloon on June 25, 1979 with "0" zero hours, still factory wrapped.'

'I had talked my neighbours into going halves initially. Within a short time, I bought them out and they purchased their own balloon.

15 FEBRUARY, 1982 - A FROZEN LAKE IN MINNESOTA, USA

'The flight across the lake covered a distance of 22 miles.'

7 SEPTEMBER, 1982 - A TETHERED FIRST RIDE

Glen taking his two-week old son, Daniel on his first ride.

1 JULY, 1984 – DISAPPEARING DAYLIGHT

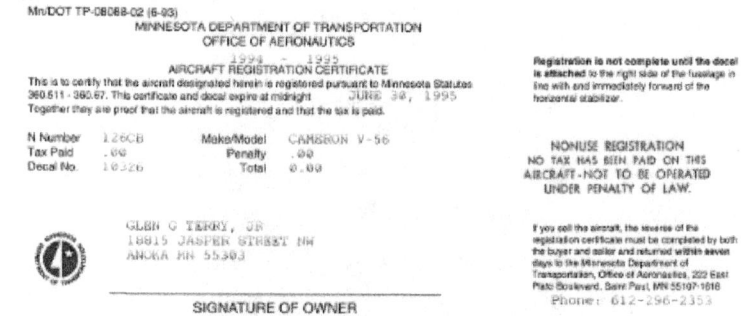

1994-1995 – AIRCRAFT NONUSE REGISTRATION CERTIFICATE

'I kept the balloon in storage and registered it as "Non-Use" in the state of Minnesota, USA until I donated to the Soukup and Thomas International Balloon and Airship Museum in Mitchell, South Dakota USA. When the balloon was donated, I kept the original Oak Box Instruments and still have them.'

20 APRIL 1996 - AIRCRAFT BILL OF SALE

From: Glen Terry

To: Soukup and Thomas International and Airship Museum, South Dakota, USA.

(When the Soukup and Thomas International Balloon and Airship Museum in Mitchell, South Dakota USA closed the basket was sold or donated to the Albuquerque Balloon Museum.)

Photos and accompanying copy from Glen Terry: The photos submitted by Glen Terry provide evidence of his ownership of his first balloon known Flamebuoyant as well as some lovely shots. He has asked that he be acknowledged as their source when being used for any publication.

∧∧∧∧∧∧∧∧∧∧∧∧∧∧∧∧∧∧∧∧∧∧∧∧∧∧∧∧∧∧∧∧

Cameron Balloons and the Royal School for the Blind Workshops' connection

Cameron Balloons was established in Bristol in 1971 by Don Cameron.

Don Cameron subsequently spoke on Radio Bristol on 20 June, 2017 confirming that Cameron Balloons obtained their baskets from the Royal School for the Blind workshops during their first 10 years. He added that some of the baskets were really big. However, the workshops discovered that by using machine tools they could do business requiring less subsidy. So, then it was necessary for Cameron Balloons to go elsewhere.

∧∧∧∧∧∧∧∧∧∧∧∧∧∧∧∧∧∧∧∧∧∧∧∧∧∧∧∧∧∧∧∧∧

Bristol Royal Workshops for the Blind

The Bristol Royal Workshops for the Blind, Park Street, Bristol would have produced gondolas for Cameron's probably when they first started in 1971. The Workshops remained in Park Street until the 1980s when they moved to South Liberty Lane.

∧∧∧∧∧∧∧∧∧∧∧∧∧∧∧∧∧∧∧∧∧∧∧∧∧∧∧∧∧∧∧∧∧

Final location for the Royal School for the Blind in Bristol

The fourth and last location of the Royal School for the Blind in Bristol was purpose-built in Henleaze, Bristol. Building was started in 1909 and opened in 1911.

EARLY 1950S – ROYAL SCHOOL FOR THE BLIND, HENLEAZE

There was only one photo in colour that we have seen of the school. It was taken by one of the former pupils, Graham Joyner in the early 1950s with his box camera.

BLUE PLAQUE FOR BRISTOL ROYAL SCHOOL FOR THE BLIND

Graham Joyner was also instrumental with a small group of pupils in arranging for a blue plaque to be placed on the boundary wall by the dual carriageway in Henleaze Road in 2012.

∧∧∧∧∧∧∧∧∧∧∧∧∧∧∧∧∧∧∧∧∧∧∧∧∧∧∧∧∧∧∧∧∧

THE HISTORY OF GOLDEN HILL FROM THE 1970s

Since the publication of The Henleaze Book in the early 1990s, the archives of Sylvia Kelly who sadly died in 2016 have been merged with those of Veronica Bowerman. Sylvia Kelly produced a Tribute to Golden Hill (1987) which was included in The Henleaze Book – see website for more details **https://www.henleazebook.com/**

Thanks to these archives we are now able to produce some further information on Golden Hill which is located in North Bristol adjacent to Bishopston, Westbury Park, Henleaze and Horfield.

Since the 1970s the amount of open space on Golden Hill has been reduced as a result of changing needs. We have also been in touch with various organisations in the area for feedback about the planning applications.

From the 1930s - Bristol Cathedral School had occupied the Golden Hill site when there were only 180 pupils.

As far back as the late 1950s - Bristol Grammar School decided that their Golden Hill playing fields were inadequate. From 1962 the school was operating from two sites – Golden Hill and Failand – approximately 4 miles apart.

In the 1970s - Bristol City Council were seeking to finalise the development of the former playing fields for Clifton Rugby Club and Q.E.H off Eastfield Road at Westbury on Trym as well. Local residents there protested at the lack of consultation, highlighted the conserved area of Westbury village and requested that any layout took full account of the special character and needs in an already overcrowded area.

In 1973 - The Henleaze Neighbourhood Society (now The Henleaze Society) was formed by local residents over concern with the continuing loss of open space in the area for housing development and a need to monitor and improve the quality of life in the locality. Many families in the area were also looking at ways to stop the development of Golden Hill playing fields, one of the last remaining open spaces in the city.

The Golden Hill playing fields involved in the early 1970s were being used by the YMCA, Bristol Cathedral School and Bristol Grammar School and totalled 37 acres (15 hectares).

Both schools had increased their number of pupils by the 1970s.

Bristol Cathedral School now had more than 400 pupils and the number of sports undertaken had diversified. They had long been trying to acquire larger sports fields and for convenience to stay in the same area.

Bristol Grammar School, particularly when it became co-educational, had also increased their number of pupils so a decision was taken to centralise their recreation activities at Failand. It was not practical for them to maintain two sites 6.5kms (four miles) apart. Their Golden Hill playing facilities had now become surplus to requirements, so the School sought professional advice on how this land might be better utilised.

October 1973 - two applications for planning permission to develop playing fields on Golden Hill from Bristol Municipal Charities and from the Governors of Bristol Cathedral School were submitted.

Following the 1973 planning permission to develop the 22.5 acres (9.1 hectares) Bristol Grammar School and the 6.2 acres (2.5 hectares) Bristol Cathedral playing fields it was reported in the Evening Post on 9 March, 1974 that planners had approved the scheme.

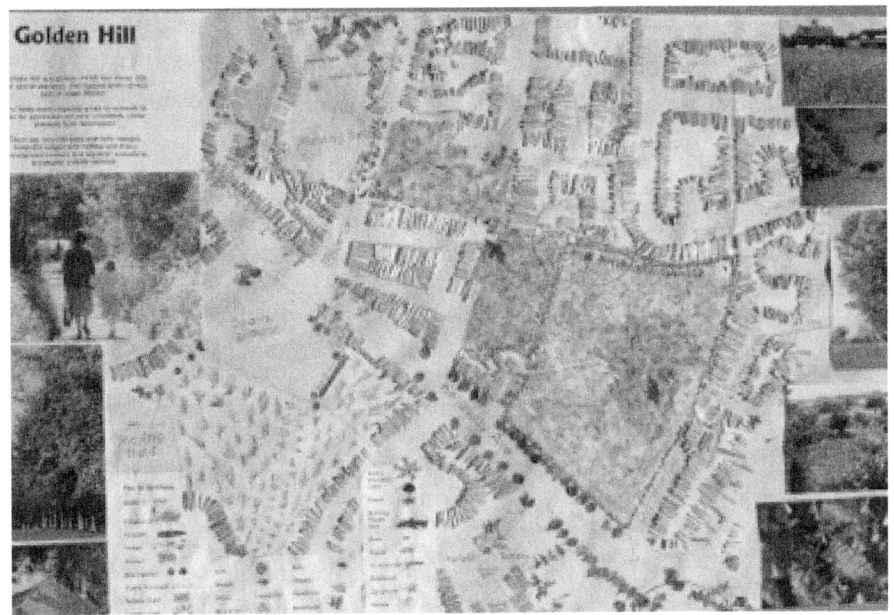

GOLDEN HILL MAP

This map was created by Sylvia Kelly from locally sourced materials. It was shown at various parish maps exhibitions, at local schools as well as local planning enquiries about Golden Hill. It was so highly praised that the Natural History Museum in Kensington also had it on show. It is now framed and looked after by a local resident.

By April, 1974 - Bristol City Council, applied for a CPO (compulsory purchase order) of the land for housing development for the people of Bristol where housing was needed. However, the new Avon County Council later rejected the applications by Bristol Municipal Charities and Bristol Cathedral School and 'The Battle of Golden Hill' followed.

22 July, 1974 – Henleaze Neighbourhood Society had distributed 2,500 questionnaires in the Henleaze area. A total of 825 questionnaires were returned which provided the following results to the questions.

561 – no housing, 256 – some housing, 8 – maximum housing, 431 - public park/playing fields, 129 - sports centre, 114 - comprehensive school, 106 - health centre 46 - community centre, 33 for allotments.

July, 1975 - as this land battle gathered momentum GHRA (Golden Hill Residents' Association) was formed. It was solely dedicated to keeping Golden Hill as open space.

At that time both Bristol Grammar School and Bristol Cathedral School sites on Golden Hill were in private ownership with limited access to outside bodies.

Tuesday, 22 July, 1975 - a public inquiry was held, into the appeal by Bristol City Council against the refusal by Avon County Council to permit the development of housing of 28.86 acres (11.7 hectares) of land on Golden Hill currently used by Bristol Grammar School and Bristol Cathedral School for playing fields.

The outcome of the public inquiry was that the appeal by Bristol City Council was dismissed and the compulsory purchase order was not confirmed. The application by the YMCA for 28 houses was also turned down by the Secretary of State.

September, 1976 – the controversial plan to build 300 homes on Golden Hill was turned down – just over a year after the planning appeal. The hopes of Bristol Grammar School, and Bristol Cathedral School to sell off their unwanted playing fields were dashed by the government ruling by Peter Shore, the Environment Secretary, that the land on Golden Hill could not be developed.

1977 - the YMCA received outline planning permission for residential development of 46 houses of some 3 acres (1.2 hectares) on the part of their extended playing fields with frontages on to Ridgehill. In 1978 the development known as Golden Park covered the remainder of Ridgehill and a new road, Sates Way was completed.

SO ON TO THE MID-1980s ......

October, 1985 – new plans from Bristol Municipal Charities who owned the Grammar School playing fields and Bristol Cathedral School that included housing went on show at the Grammar School pavilion on Golden Hill.

1986 - the YMCA on adjoining fields submitted a planning application for houses and all-weather playing pitch. However, by November that year Avon County Council had rejected the two schemes relating to the YMCA playing fields and the Bristol Grammar and Cathedral schools and because of concerns over the additional traffic that would be generated and because the proposals were contrary to the County Council's Structure Plan.

May, 1986 - at the invitation of Bristol Municipal Charities GHRA attended a meeting at their headquarters on 22 May concerning the Bristol Grammar School playing fields at Golden Hill. Bristol Municipal Charities advised and confirmed in their proposal document that they were examining how the land might be used. They advised that pupils from the Grammar School would no longer be playing there from the end of the summer term. The GHRA were not happy with their proposals.

No operator for the proposed supermarket on Golden Hill had been chosen at this stage.

1986. Friday, 6 June, and Sunday, 8 June - an exhibition organised by Bristol Municipal Charities about the plans for a new housing development and a new supermarket went on show to the public at Bristol Grammar School's pavilion, Golden Hill. The application was anticipated to go before the City's planning committee late in September.

1986, 25 June – in view of the interest and concern that the proposals would raise the June exhibition the 11th AGM of Golden Hill Residents' Association was changed from 29 June to a larger venue at Henleaze Junior School. It was attended by some 150 members including councillors Joyce Fey and Robert Trench. Both were adamant that building a supermarket and housing on the 29 acres of playing fields currently used by Bristol Grammar School and Bristol Cathedral School on Golden Hill sites must be opposed. Members at the meeting were unanimous in retaining the area as playing fields.

1986, August - Henleaze Neighbourhood Society urged people to oppose the controversial Golden Hill development for a supermarket and housing as soon as possible. Leaflets were sent out to residents in the area highlighting the likely problems that could ensue.

1986, September - the YMCA on adjoining fields submitted a planning application for houses and all-weather playing pitch.

1986, 7 November - Avon County Council rejected the two schemes relating to Bristol Grammar and Cathedral schools and the YMCA playing fields because of concerns over the additional traffic that would be generated and because the proposals were contrary to the County Council's Structure Plan. They issued a directive to Bristol City Council that permission to develop should be refused.

1986, 19 November - before this Bristol City Council meeting – the Secretary of State decided to take the issue out of Bristol City Council's hands because of the possible effect on the area and its impact on nearby shopping centres. The two plans are now being determined by the Secretary of State.

1987, 2 June - Proposed development of YMCA playing fields for housing – GHRA asked people to attend the inquiry and also to write to the Department of Environment to register their views. The inquiry was subsequently postponed at the request of the YMCA.

1987, November - The Henleaze Neighbourhood Society thanked all who had completed their Questionnaire, distributed to residents in April 1987 relating to both the YMCA and Bristol Municipal and Cathedral School outline planning permission applications. Henleaze Neighbourhood Society confirmed that the information had been collated in readiness for the public enquiry. Readers were urged to send in individual letters expressing their views to the Department of Environment and also to attend the public inquiry on 15 December.

A bulletin was delivered to Golden Hill Residents' Association members asking them to turn up at the Public Inquiry in December relating to the Playing Fields used by Bristol Grammar and Bristol Cathedral Schools for a proposed supermarket and housing. Readers were also asked to complete a tear off slip about existing shopping facilities in the area to provide evidence about whether or not there was a need for a superstore at Golden Hill.

1987, 15 – 23 December - an Inspector acting for the Secretary of State held the local public inquiry into the proposed supermarket complex on part of the former Bristol Grammar School playing fields and the proposed housing development on the Cathedral School playing field.

Attendees were informed that the siting of a modern supermarket on Golden Hill would not only be an asset but would enhance the historic area of Henleaze. Andrew Larman, for Golden Hill Residents' Association said that 'a superstore on the site would be nothing else but wholly disruptive and visually intrusive.' He also reported that 98.2 of the residents who responded to the Golden Hill Residents' Association questionnaire were satisfied with current shopping facilities. Others who opposed the scheme included Joyce Fey and Bob Trench, local tory councillors as well as Jerry Hicks, chairman of the Bristol Sports Association. 700 letters of objection had been received by the inspector and the two councils.

1987, 23 December - the Inspector, Mr F Cosgrove, who held the local inquiry from 15-23 December made his usual site inspection accompanied by representatives of the Applicants, the Councils, GHRA, HNS, and other interested parties.

1988, February – Golden Hill Residents' Association thanked its members for turning up at the Inquiry, writing letters of objection and displaying in their windows 'Hand off Golden Hill' posters. They were asked to remove the poster, but to retain the latter in case of need at a later date.

1988, 5 July - following the Public Inquiry in December, 1987 Nicholas Ridley, the Secretary of State issued a letter indicating that he was disposed to accept his inspector's recommendation to accept the application, subject to completion of a legal agreement between the applicants and the city council to ensure public access to the new/improved sports facilities. These details were discussed between the parties and agreement was sealed on 5 December 1988.

Tesco Stores Ltd subsequently purchased the site with outline planning permission from Bristol Municipal Charities and submitted a full application for approval.

1988 – YMCA PLAYING FIELDS

1989, 19 January – the Secretary of State, Nicholas Ridley issued his decision letter granting outline planning permission to the applicants Bristol Municipal Charities and Bristol Cathedral School for Application No1953P/86N which included the formation of an access road leading off Kellaway Avenue opposite Horfield Common and the construction of a Class 1 superstore of 55,000 sq. ft gross floor area with associated car park and service area on that part of the Bristol Municipal Charities Playing fields adjoining Kellaway Avenue and Lansdown Terrace on a 6.5 acre (2.54 hectares) site.

The application also included:

Outline permission showing means of access only to the development which consisted the Class 1 retail store

Playing fields on the remaining on the remaining 16.08 acres (6.51 hectares) to include an all-weather surface, replacement of the two existing pavilions and an implement shed by a new pavilion with ancillary residential accommodation and an implement shed.

Residential development on the 6.28 acres (2.54 hectares) of the Bristol Cathedral playing field.

Formation of the new access road and junction to serve the proposed uses, entailing the removal of mature lime trees set within the pavement on the west side of Kellaway Avenue.

Landscaping within the above area.

1989, 4 -7 April - a local public Inquiry was held from regarding the proposed development of the YMCA playing field. Following rejection of the plans by the Environment Secretary, Chris Patten to build on its remaining six acres (2.4 hectares) of playing fields GHRA (Golden Hill Residents' Association) contacted the YMCA asking them to keep in touch with their future intentions and received an encouraging reply.

1989, September – Golden Hill Residents' Association ascertained that the Bristol Municipal Charities upgrade and floodlighting application for the remaining ground on the Bristol Grammar School field had been withdrawn. It was later replaced with new plans which included the likely demolition of the Clocktower Pavilion. The solicitors acting on behalf of Bristol Municipal Charities indicated that their client had declined to enter into a planning agreement to include floodlighting and therefore the work could not go ahead until the City Clerk reached a conclusion. When permission had been granted by Nicholas Ridley there was an important proviso that the public (i.e. the Club) must be given access in order to compensate for the loss of part of the existing playing area.

1989, 22 December - the Bristol Observer announced that 'plans were now in hand by Tesco to build a supermarket on adjoining land used by Bristol Grammar and Cathedral Schools.

1990, February - the plans for building houses on the YMCA playing field were rejected by the Minister but, following the April,

1989 Inquiry. Golden Hill Residents' Association contacted the YMCA asking them to keep in touch with their future intentions and again a positive response was forthcoming.

1990, March - a public meeting organised by Golden Hill Residents' Association was held at Henleaze Infant School on 7 March in connection with the proposed development by Tesco Supermarket of part of the Golden Hill playing fields. This was an opportunity to meet local councillors and representatives from Tesco, in order to voice opinion and to ask any relevant questions.

The school hall was filled to capacity with many standing all evening. The audience included many members, non-members, local retailers, local councillors as well as a team of approximately 12 from Tesco, although only two spoke on behalf of the retailer.

A significant number of letters were received by Tesco following this meeting.

1990, April, - following the March meeting a petition with 3,970 signatures was completed by many members, non-members, local retailers and friends. This petition of support for Councillor Arthur Keefe was presented on one long sheet measuring 150 feet (45.72 metres) to Avon County Council in preparation for the meeting of their Traffic & Highways Committee on 1 June. The petition recommended that the Tesco's application be sent back to Chris Patten. It was hoped that Bristol City Council would do the same at their meeting on 8 August.

1990, June - Avon Committee agreed to urge Chris Patten, the Environment Secretary, to reverse an earlier decision and to refuse Tesco permission to build on Golden Hill, Avon CC agreed to ask Bristol City Council to join in the protest.

1990, June – Golden Hill Residents' Association had been in touch with Ed Allingham from the YMCA with a view to collaborating on ways to use their facilities (playing field and pavilion) for the general benefit of the community.

1990, 14 July - a demonstration was staged on Kellaway Avenue on this Saturday in order to show what traffic chaos could do to the area in a very short space of time. A large number of friends, with babies, children, prams etc. turned up and a good time was had by all as they crossed and re-crossed Kellaway Avenue en-masse which kept the traffic at bay for short periods. Many 'beeps' from passing motorists indicated support. Television and press were present.

1990, 8 August - report by the Bristol City Planning Office on Golden Hill published.

1990, 10 August - the Bristol Mercury reported that Tesco had put forward revised plans so that only six of the Kellaway Avenue trees would be axed and that efforts would be made to screen the store from residents living in nearby Lansdown Terrace.

1990, 27 August - an article from David Harrison of Bristol Post headed 'D-day looms at last for the battle fields.' He included the headline on the same area that appeared in their publication 17 years ago on 16 March 1973.

1990, by October - it was reported that the Bristol Grammar School pavilion had been severely vandalised on several occasions whilst awaiting demolition.

1991, 17 April - this Bristol City Planning Committee meeting was attended by five members of the committee of GHRA as observers and listeners only. The Committee agreed to defer a final decision on the Tesco's application until the Avon County Council meeting on 3 May. The Chairman did point out that they were 'reaching the end of the road' and highlighted the problems that such a long delay in reaching a decision could bring. It also appeared that the present secretary of State, Chris Patten would be unlikely to revoke the original planning permission agreed by the former Secretary of State, Nicholas Ridley. If Bristol City Council revoked planning consent they could be liable to pay millions of pounds in compensation to Tesco with little hope of aid from Central Government.

1991, May - the YMCA met local interested, residents, parents etc. met in order to form a much-needed youth Club in the Henleaze area, the intention being to base the club in the former cricket pavilion.

1991, 16 May – 16 June - travellers arrived in May but departed in June making it quite difficult for some of the residents in the properties surrounding Golden Hill. Tesco confirmed, in writing, to Sylvia Kelly of the Henleaze Neighbourhood Society that they had applied to the Court for an order for possession to remove the travellers who subsequently left the site, including the pavilion, in a very bad state. Heavy equipment was need to clear the rubbish. The site was made more secure.

1991, Summer - GHRA announced that there was to be a meeting between Avon and Bristol Councils soon and it was hoped that Tesco would also attend. Several written questions had been submitted by GHRA confirming their continuing opposition to the development on Golden Hill.

Protestors set up a 24-hour vigil, blocked the entry of contractors on to the site and occupied the gate area. Ye Olde Green Tea caravan provided refreshment. Protestors were spurred on by a conservationists' victory in Stroud three years previously in which the local council had wanted to fell 12 beech trees to improve access to a new Tesco store. Roped to the trees in an all-night vigil, the protesters had managed to stop them being felled. The Golden Hill protesters were also given hope by Bristol West MP William Waldegrave, who backed their actions despite Tesco having planning permission.

For most of June, the "campers" managed to bar officials and workmen from entering the site, but by the end of the month Tesco had had enough and applied for a possession order at the High Court.

1991, 4 September - Bristol planners met and finally granted Tesco's their full planning permission to build, subject to certain conditions.

1991, Winter - two subsidiary planning applications were launched by Bristol Municipal Charities for housing development on the original Bristol Cathedral playing field for 61 terraced, semi and detached houses on the greater part of the site plus open spaces, footpaths, roads, etc. Golden Hill Residents' Association were concerned about these properties using the same access road with Tesco. A second application was also submitted for 9 semi and detached houses on the greater part of the site on the same field, but fronting Brookland Road. The splitting of the development was a departure from the original plan. The original plan for proposed sheltered accommodation was also dropped.

1992, May - Tesco obtained detailed planning permission for the development of a store on Golden Hill. The store is sited on 6.5 acres (2.63 hectares) of land that were formerly part of Bristol Grammar School playing fields. To the rear of the store is Lansdown Terrace, to the side Kellaway Avenue with a new road access subsequently included and known as Lime Trees Road.

1992, June - local people as well as the Planning Committee were appalled by the decision from Nicholas Ridley, the Environment Secretary to allow the go-ahead for a supermarket, plus a small estate of houses on a nearby 14-acre sire owned by Bristol Cathedral School and Bristol Municipal charities. Protesters were soon on the scene setting up camp in an effort to stop the application.

A JCB digger had to turn back from the site of the proposed new Tesco store. More than 70 residents had blocked its way.

Eight protesters chained themselves to the gates at the entrance. They were part of 150 plus group of protesters who had gathered from early morning at the Golden Hill site. Many of them had slept on the land opposite overnight.

Contractors abandoned attempts to chop down five trees on Golden Hill as protestors had staged a treetop sit-in.

Local residents and conservationists met with Tesco chiefs and the contractors. Tesco agreed not to carry out any further work until its directors had discussed proposals by local people to keep open the site. Residents were asked to take down posters at the site as their part of the bargain. Tesco asked for a halt of all protests while the plans were being studied.

William Waldegrave, MP met local people in a house on Golden Hill one evening. He was honest enough to say that he did not hold out a great deal of hope at this stage, but added that 'while there's life, there's hope.'

GOLDEN HILL CAMPAIGN BADGES

These badges are from the Sylvia Kelly collection and were worn by many during the Golden Hill Campaign.

1992, 27 June - a Chain of Hope, a human chain of approximately 2,500 people of all ages encircled the Golden Hill to highlight its many friends and its need for more.

1992, July - after 64 days of protest, the bulldozers rolled in to a storm of protest, narrowly missing two protesters who had chained themselves to a skip at the site. Tesco and Bristol Municipal Charities had taken protestors to court for repossession of the whole field. Some of the protestors were singing 'Land of Hope and Glory' and 'Lord of the Dance' as they peacefully walked off scattering bunches of carnations and roses on the pavement as they went. More than three vans of police officers and four mounted policemen were waiting in nearby Dyrham Close as the under-sheriff of Avon, John Grenfell at 10.30am gave notice to the protestors that they were being removed from the site. Some of the protestors were arrested and charged whilst attempting to delay the convoy of lorries with portacabins entering the site.

Other options and possible sites, other than Golden Hill, for the proposed Tesco Supermarket were considered by Tesco, Bristol City Council, GHRA, Bristol Rain Forest Group, William Waldegrave and others but no agreement was reached. In August, Sylvia Kelly and others received a letter from Tesco acknowledging correspondence concerning the development by Tesco and Bristol Municipal Charities. It advised that unfortunately no viable alternative had emerged.

1992, 5 August - Tesco took out a one-page advert in the Evening Post to set out some facts, put their case, and to defend their reputation as an environmentally aware and sensitive company. It was entitled 'Golden Hill. After two years of assumptions, subjectivity and name calling, something new. The facts.'

In order to defend their reputation as an environmentally friendly company Tesco highlighted the history of the planning applications. Bristol Grammar School had sold their part of Golden Hill in the 1980s and in a short space of time the fields became seriously neglected. Bristol Municipal Charities and Bristol Cathedral School applied for planning permission for 6.5 acres (2.6 hectares) of Golden Hill for a Class 1 superstore which was granted by the Secretary of State for the Environment.

Tesco emphasised that they bought the 6.5 acres (2.6 hectares) part of the playing fields only after outline planning permission for had been granted. The previous owners of the remaining 16.1 acres (6.51 hectares) then had funding. Tesco outlined the ways that they would help these owners by building drains, relevelling the land, laying out of four rugby pitches, a football pitch and a cricket pitch plus building a fully illuminated all-weather playing surface and a new pavilion.

The advert gave details of Tesco's aims that included blending in with the environment by using local stones, bricks and slates where possible for the building; the store to be fully landscaped using more than 200 mature trees, which included 40 semi-mature, plus 20,000 shrubs and flowers.

Tesco ended the advert by underlining that they really cared not only about the environment, but also about people and thanking those who had taken the trouble to read their side about Golden Hill.

1992, 14 August - in the afternoon protesters' screams, weeping and chants turned to an eerie silence as contractors moved in to saw down four of the lime trees in Kellaway Avenue to provide access to the proposed Tesco store. Last-ditch legal efforts to stop the development had failed at 1pm. Campaigners in the 89-year-old limes - some had been there for 24 hours - were told to come down for their own safety. After 84 days of protest the law was out in force.

Three hundred angry campaigners on the opposite pavement faced 100 police, including some on horseback.

1992, 15 August - the Independent reported that after a 24-hour vigil lasting more than 80 days men, women and children wept after their efforts to save a row of four lime trees from being felled to make way for the proposed new supermarket had failed.

Tesco issued a statement saying that the trees would be replaced by 40 semi-mature limes plus 20,000 other trees, shrubs and plants.

'The Battle of Golden Hill' was over.

1992, 19 August – an advertisement in the Evening Post outlined why Golden Hill needed more friends to continue the campaign to stop Tesco developing on Golden Hill and other green field sites.

1992, September – there was a national day of action against Tesco. A TV documentary was shown on Channel 4 about superstore planning issues and featured footage from the Golden Hill campaign.

1992, October – during the first Saturday of the month 28 Tesco stores, including eight in London held Golden Hill protests.

1992, 27 November - the Evening Post stated that 'A group is being set up to give people more say on the development of Tesco's controversial new store in Golden Hill, Bristol' The initiative was taken by MP William Waldegrave, Avon County councillor, John Portch and Tesco property estates director Nigel Burton. A Tesco spokesperson said 'It has always been our intention to build bridges with the Henleaze community.'

1992, 7 – 31 December - an exhibition of paintings, photographs and poetry from locals who opposed Tesco's bid to build a superstore on Golden Hill went on show at Bristol Central Library. Included were sketches by local artist Rachel Sawko who had followed the events at Golden Hill over the years, photos from Simon Chapman taken during the summer demonstrations and poems by Pat West, Isabelle Gifford and Rosemary Quinnell.

1993, February - the liaison group set up by Tesco and local representatives in November 1992 produced a community newsletter containing the latest information about the Tesco/Bristol Municipal Charities development at Kellaway Avenue. It also included Avon County and Bristol City contacts for readers to raise any points for their next meeting with Tesco.

1993, Tuesday, 25 May - the newly built Tesco, Golden Hill, opened its doors to the public.

1994 – A projected figure of new supermarkets opening per year in the UK for the three main supermarkets was given by GHRA as 100 with many on green field sites like Golden Hill. They suggested to their members that a boycott of Tesco, Golden Hill could help reduce this figure.

1995 – Tesco requested a variation on condition 12 of their planning permission to allow them to open on Sundays which was subsequently granted, in spite of some opposition locally from residents.

From the early 1970s until 1992 - other organisations besides the Henleaze Neighbourhood Society and Golden Hill Residents' Association that were involved in the attempt to retain Golden Hill as open space included: Henleaze Traders' Association, Bristol & West Grocers' Association, The Sports Council, (South West Region), Bristol Sports' Association, Bristol Civic Society, Avon Wildlife Trust, The Avon Lawn Tennis Association, Ardagh Sports Club and Ardagh Ladies Bowling Club.

2018 - The aftermath

It can be seen from these comments how these playing fields have taken on a different mantle in the last 25 years.

Helen Furber, Chairperson of The Henleaze Society

Helen issued the following statement:

Concerns about the future of the Golden Hill playing fields led local residents to discuss the need to have a local amenity society to collate local views on planning and other matters in the Henleaze area. This led to the establishment of The Henleaze Society (formerly The Henleaze Neighbourhood Society) in 1973. The society formed an executive committee and recruited volunteers to distribute information letters.

Over the years the society's trustees and volunteers have worked with and for the local community to ensure that Henleaze is a good place in which to live and work. Key priorities have been developed; they include:

Monitoring local planning applications and, where appropriate, working with members to support or object to applications. To support the society's ongoing work, the society worked with Bristol City Council to publish 'Henleaze: Our Place Character Appraisal' in 2016.

Helping to improve the local environment. Examples of the society's work are time spent developing Old Quarry Park to meet the needs of the community, arranging for hanging baskets and flower troughs to be planted in Henleaze Road and Wellington Hill West and assisting with street issues such as poor lighting and removing graffiti. Street benches have also been provided in Henleaze Road.

Each year four hard copy newsletters are hand delivered to members by volunteers. In addition, the Society has purchased and updates four notice boards, has a website and issues electronic updates.

Organising events such as an open gardens day, annual trips, lunches and talks.

Providing and maintaining a public access defibrillator.

Liaising with local councillors, the police and other organisations.

The society has grown substantially since 1973. Membership is per household and, as at November 2018, is £5 a year if you live in Henleaze (£7.50 if the newsletters are posted to you).

Up to date joining information is available by sending an email to

ths.newsletter@gmail.com

or from the society's noticeboards.

Martin Ashley, Chairman of GHRA from 1997

Martin issued this statement:

GHRA – Golden Hill Resident's Association was formed in July 1975 as a result of possible loss of open space within the City of Bristol. Three local playing field sites were highlighted on Golden Hill. Two fenced off fields were being used by local schools Bristol Grammar and Bristol Cathedral. The third was the YMCA ground surrounded by local housing.

The association is still in existence but is not active at present.

Since the late 1990s the Association has helped several local causes including the purchase of oak trees for Project Ardagh and help with fundraising for Golden Hill Cricket Club. Martin Ashley continues as Chairman and can be contacted by email

martin.ashley@btinternet.com

Gareth Williams, Manager of Tesco, Golden Hill

Gareth provided the following information:

Customers - Tesco at Limes Trees Road now serves up to

25,000 customers a week, we are constantly trying to improve our range to serve our customer better.

Colleagues - we give employment to 200 plus colleagues, more at seasonal times and we have given lots of opportunities for those struggling to find work through the Princes Trust and Movement to Work schemes.

Charity- through the community food connection programme we have given away the equivalent of over 7865 meal this year (2018) so far.

Through the 'Bags for Help scheme 38 projects have benefited a share of £135,000. We are also a main collection point for the Trussell Trust food bank.

(2018 marks 25 years of trading by Tesco on Golden Hill.)

Golden Hill Playing Fields

Golden Hill Playing Fields, accessed from Lime Trees Road, are owned by Bristol Grammar School. Bristol Rovers Football Club took out a 20-year lease in 2001 and then Redland High School for Girls took an assignment of the existing lease from Rovers in 2004 until the school merged with Redmaids in 2016/17 at which time and, as a consequence, the new Redmaids' High School inherited the lease. The site is approximately 14 acres.

These vastly improved pitches include three full sized grass pitches, and one full sized artificial sand dressed floodlit pitch. The brick pavilion to the left, when entering the playing fields from Lime Trees Road, provides changing, equipment storage facilities etc. It was built at the same time as the Tesco store and replaced the former Bristol Grammar and Bristol Cathedral school buildings demolished in early 1990s which had been used for these purposes.

The Golden Hill Sports Ground

Golden Hill Sports (GHS), accessed from Wimbledon Road, was established in 2007 as a legal entity to enable the ground to be purchased from Bristol YMCA Inc.

The money to do this came from a combination grants from several sporting and environmental bodies, generous donations from a number of local residents plus past and present cricket members and finally, a significant loan from the English Cricket Board (ECB)

As a way of saying thank you and building closer links to all those in the locality that supported us whilst at the same time raising funds to help us repay the loan, the then Chair of GHS, Chris Drew, came up with the idea of 'Party in the Park' (PITP) - a community fair held on the playing fields on a Saturday afternoon in September with a range of live music, demonstrations, stalls & attractions open for all the family to come and enjoy.

PITP has proved extremely popular over the years and is a key factor in turning us into a club for the community rather than just the cricket club we were when GHS first out.

The cricket club is still central to this community involvement especially as a result of the thriving youth section and the more recent introduction of a rapidly growing girls cricket section alongside the ladies and long-established men's' teams.

The link up with Golden Hill Sonics a few years ago who use the ground for youth football during the winter has further strengthened the community bonds as have the local bridge clubs **http://www.woebc.co.uk/** who play in the pavilion on several weekday afternoons and evenings.

2017 saw us complete the repayment of the ECB loan and also replace the old wooden balcony on the pavilion. This was again with help of the community who voted for us in very large numbers to enable us to secure a monetary award from a national insurance company.

Our attention is now focused on some much-needed renovation work on the inside of the 50+ year old pavilion to bring it up to modern day standards which we hope will be to the benefit of club members and the wider community.

Footnote about Keith Milsom who kindly provided the above information.

For more details see the website:

http://www.goldenhillsports.com/

'Our fantastic completed balcony gives the clubhouse a new lease of life!

'On 17th June, 2018 a special celebration took place to officially name the clubhouse the Keith Milsom Pavilion. Surrounded by players past and present and three generations of his family, Keith was rightly honoured in his 50th year with the club. And the opportunity to honour one of our longest serving members. In his typical humble fashion, Keith told the Evening Post that he thought the club might name a bin after him, due to his habit of tidying up after everyone.

'We're pleased to say that Keith continues to accumulate runs on the pitch and to earn respect from everyone associated with the club. He's a YM legend who sets a shining example of what a true club member should be.

Residential development

61 properties were built to the rear of Tesco in a new road known as The Furlong during the 1990s plus others fronting adjacent

Brookland Road.

Michael Stephenson, Harbury Road resident

Michael Stephenson adds:

'Tesco Golden Hill put the final boot into the local shops in Harbury Road that is for sure; just the ongoing change in shopping habits I am afraid. When we moved here in 1980 the Co-op was active as well as a laundrette and as you say newsagents and a fruit and veg shop which also sold fresh fish! Our daughter Erika had a Saturday job there in the mid-1980s involving weighing out mud covered potatoes. The newsagent was well used and they provided newspaper deliveries for morning and evening and the lads' bikes were all over the path at delivery times.

'The Co-op was handy of course for the little forgotten things but could not survive in the end. Another loss in more recent times was the closure of the post office on the corner of Wellington Hill West and Cransley Crescent which still thrives however as a corner shop, now as McColls, despite Tesco and Waitrose.'

Final comment

The Guardian reported the following on 27 August, 2011:

https://www.theguardian.com/politics/2011/aug/27/councils-greenfield-sites-planning-proposals

'The shake-up of England's planning laws is likely to result in more development on greenfield sites, but this will not happen without the approval of local communities, according to the government department responsible for the reforms.

'The national planning policy framework, a consultation document published three weeks ago, has provoked consternation in the ranks of

the National Trust and the Council for the Protection of Rural England. The campaign groups claim the framework dispenses with the previous government's emphasis that developers should build primarily on brownfield, urban sites rather than greenfield sites at the edge of the countryside.'

∧∧∧∧∧∧∧∧∧∧∧∧∧∧∧∧∧∧∧∧∧∧∧∧∧∧∧∧∧∧∧∧∧∧

HENLEAZE BOWLING CLUB (1928-1978) - THE FIRST 50 YEARS

Henleaze Bowling Club was founded in 1928, when Clarence Davey purchased land opposite his house in Grange Court Road and, with some friends, set about forming a bowling club. The club was incorporated on 14th June 1928 as a limited company. The cost of laying the green was approximately £600. A wooden pavilion was built on the site of the present car park, along with a shed (presumably for green-keeping tools) for a total of £520.

JUNE, 1928, GREEN OPENING BY LORD MAYOR, ALDERMAN DOWLING

Between 1929 and 1938 lockers were leased to club members at 5/- (five shillings, 25p) pa (per annum).

1931 - cash was raised from the membership to purchase a shelter; this was sold for £15 in 1939.

1936 - Henleaze Bowling Club, originally a member of the Somerset BA, transferred affiliation to Gloucestershire BA and at the same time became a founder member at the formation of the City and County of Bristol Bowling Association.

1939, 10 May - the new Pavilion was completed and presented to the club as a gift from two of the founders, Clarence himself and Charles Setter. It was opened by the President of the EBA, Harry Thompson. The original pavilion was removed, sold for £20, and the car park made at a cost of £300.

1939 – CELEBRATION OF NEW PAVILION

1940 - silver spoons costing 3/3d (16.25p) each were presented as prizes on "rinks evenings" - what were latterly known as "spoons nights". Both before and after the war, a cleaner was employed to keep the clubhouse clean and decoration and repair of the club house was by a paid contractor.

1946 - JW "Robbie" Robison was awarded his International "cap", a wonderful honour for himself and the club. He had already been a member of Gloucestershire's Middleton Cup winning team of 1936, the Bath Open Pairs in 1937, the Gloucestershire County Pairs in 1939, Weston Open Pairs, CCBBA Pairs and Rinks in 1940. In 1945 he was runner-up in the EBA singles, Captain of Gloucestershire, runner up in the GBA singles, and skippered the rink that won the GBA Fours. He went on to win the CCBBA pairs again in 1950.

1949 - the green was re-laid at a cost of £322, with a Special Appeal Fund set up to meet the cost. Why this should have been necessary is not recorded.

1954 - the teak benches were purchased at a cost of 14 guineas each (£14.70), with various members paying for a seat with a plate displaying the donor's name.

1954 – CAPTAIN'S DAY

1956 - the club reached the semi-final of CCBBA Inter-Club Tournament - the Clarence Davey Cup - only to be beaten by a team from Greenbank BC.

1971 – PRESIDENT'S DAY

1978 - the club celebrated the completion of 50 years in existence with a new flag - complete with the date of foundation - which was expertly hand-sewn by Alwyn Harper, who became the club's first Lady Captain in 1982.

A colour photo (shown here in black and white) was taken in 1978, the year of the Club's 50th anniversary.

SOME OF THE 43 LADIES ON THE ROTA FOR CATERING

The Club had long enjoyed excellent catering support from the wives - all matches were accompanied by a meal in those days. Members were encouraged to join as a family and wives played in matches and in Club competitions. However, it wasn't until the early 80s that the Ladies' Section, under Avery Harper, became affiliated to Gloucester Bowling Association and began playing matches in their own right. Today's Club is fully integrated with Committee positions and other roles open to all Members.

THE CLUB CELEBRATED ITS 90TH ANNIVERSARY IN 2018

Many thanks to Tom Logan of the Henleaze Bowling Club for providing the photos from their archives and the text.

For further information about the Club – see

http://www.henleazebowlingclub.org.uk/

^^^^^^^^^^^^^^^^^^^^^^^^^^^^^^^^^^^^^

OLD QUARRY PARK

There are plans to include an information board in the park showing details of its history so keep visiting to view other innovations that are currently being included for visitors – young and old.

1930s – OLD QUARRY PARK

This photo was taken before the lake was brought up to a higher level in line with Henleaze Road dual carriageway. View looking towards Eastfield Terrace. Rubble from the bombing in Bristol in World War Two was later used to achieve this.

1930s - CLARK'S YARD (JUNCTION OF HENLEAZE AND EASTFIELD ROADS

John Clark is cleaning a car in the yard.

In the background is the Clark's first home adjacent to Old Quarry Park which was built in the 1700s on the junction of Eastfield and Henleaze Roads. It was one of the oldest properties in the area, but the yard and properties were demolished in the 2012 to make way for sheltered accommodation known as Amelia Lodge.

(The two photos are courtesy of the John Clark collection)

∧∧∧∧∧∧∧∧∧∧∧∧∧∧∧∧∧∧∧∧∧∧∧∧∧∧∧∧∧∧

ST URSULA'S

A 1941 virtual walk around Henleaze taken by pupils of St Ursula's

Much has been written about the Sacred Heart Convent, Brecon Road that subsequently became known as St Ursula's - particularly in the following two publications:

Sisters of Mercy, Bristol by Jean Olwen Maynard

The Henleaze Book by Veronica Bowerman.

Up to date details on the school is now known as St Ursula's E-Act Academy can be found through this link:

https://stursulasacademy.e-act.org.uk/

However, when Sylvia Kelly, a former teacher at St Ursula's and founder of the Phoenix Hedge Preservation Group sadly died in 2016 her family asked Veronica if she would like to merge Sylvia's archives on Henleaze with hers.

https://sites.google.com/site/phoenixhedge/

For more than 40 years Veronica and Sylvia had produced many trails, walks and presentations for local schools and residents about Henleaze. Sylvia's expertise lay mainly in the flora and fauna but she was very interested in local history, particularly relating to Golden Hill. The following has been researched from their joint archives so most of this information will not have appeared beforehand in either of the publications mentioned previously.

In this particular presentation June Munday (nee Hex), a former pupil joined them for this St Ursula's event on Friday, 13 February 2009.

The aim of this virtual history event was to help the pupils remember the 1940s by highlighting the difficult times local people often encountered.

Pupils from Years five and six (10-11year olds), participated in a *Virtual Walk in Henleaze on 3 April 1941*, their local suburb in North West Bristol. The pupils were taken back in a time machine to 1941 - 68 years ago - when Henleaze was a very different place.

Many samples of items relating to WWII events in Henleaze in the 1940s were brought along by the presenters to show the children.

The presenters were pleased to see that some of the children had dressed up as evacuees but they all really entered into the spirit of the Virtual Walk presentation.

Each pupil left St Ursula's on their virtual walk to Golden Hill with June, who had been six years old in 1941. They each had to imagine that they were taking June home to tea. Some of their tasks, sights and encounters en-route were: virtually - no traffic on the road, rationing - petrol and food, purchasing items in ounces such as bacon, sugar, margarine etc. with their ration book, queues of people waiting for food, air raid sirens, air raid shelter stop, the all clear, bombed houses, an ice house at Waterdale, talking to the ARP wardens at the Crescent, seeing nurses billeted at St Margaret's School going to work to attend the wounded soldiers at Southmead Hospital, collecting milk at Claremont where their family were registered. Finally, each pupil and June were able to eat oatie biscuits (made to a 1940s recipe by Sylvia Kelly), when they arrived at their make-believe home at Golden Hill!

There were also some special sound effects to go with the presentation which included queues of people talking, air raid sirens, bombs dropping, cows mooing, dogs barking, swifts screeching, etc.

To give an even more understanding of 1941 the presenters included a visual PowerPoint presentation which included copies of posters giving instructions such as the following:

Dig for victory, don't waste food, carry your gas mask

GAS MASK FOR A BABY C1940s

We were fortunate enough to have been loaned various items for the event, including newspapers of the era, shrapnel, weighing scales, a milk carrier etc. Several of the boys were keen to try on the gas masks! Many were surprised that socks needed to be darned in 1941 - often in different colours!

Grateful thanks to local resident Julian Lea-Jones **http://www.history4u.info/** as well as Sylvia Kelly and June Munday for sourcing so many 1941 artefacts for the pupils. These items made the virtual walk so much more meaningful for them.

Local resident Bob Powles, who used to run Powles Garage in Cardigan Road, filled us in with the history of his family's nearby garage during World War Two. Bob was 90 years old in 2009, but he had some amazing memories of the 1940s.

There was also some Wartime music playing including the song purported to be the Prime Minster, Winston Churchill's favourite - Rub Rabbit Run!

The Headmistress, at that time, Mrs McNaughton attended and thanked the three presenters at the finish for making the event so interesting and memorable for the pupils.

^^^^^^^^^^^^^^^^^^^^^^^^^^^^^^^^^^^^^^

WESTBURY PARK TENNIS CLUB OVER THE YEARS

It all started when a young clergyman, Leslie Gordon Vining, came home from France after WW1 to the parish of St Alban's. He suggested the formation of a non-sectarian and non-political organisation to bring people together living in the district and particularly to extend a welcome to newcomers.

The Westbury Park Social Club came into existence in St Alban's Church hall to provide a means for people to meet together in an atmosphere of friendliness. At that time there was a varied programme which included Whist Drives, Bridge, Dances, Dramatic Performances and a variety of other entertainment. However, members of the Club soon wanted to continue their activities throughout the summer and a tennis club was suggested in the early 1920s.

The question of a purchase of a hut, its equipment and maintenance were subsequently discussed under the chairmanship of Canon Vining in September 1921. It is believed that the Club started playing tennis in 1920 and purchased the courts in 1923. In October a Sub-Committee was constituted to report on the obtaining of a ground for summer games. The land for summer games soon became a realised fact.

The Indenture dated 10 November 1923 shows that the Vendor of the land for tennis purposes was Sidney Curtis of adjacent Springfield Farm.

Trustees were appointed by the Committee of Management to facilitate the purchase of the land, adjacent to Russell Grove, on behalf of the Westbury Park Social Club. These Trustees were five local residents – Sidney Stroud, Gerald Griffiths, Reginald Baker Christopher Love and Leonard Richards.

The area Springfield Farm was updated to read Springfield Building Estate in the indenture. The pieces of land coloured dark grey on the plan were the ones purchased by the Club for lawn tennis or other games. The price paid for this land by Westbury Park Social Club was £650. During the first years just two grass courts were used but owing to the subsequent interest in tennis the number of courts increased to four grass and two hard courts to accommodate the additional members.

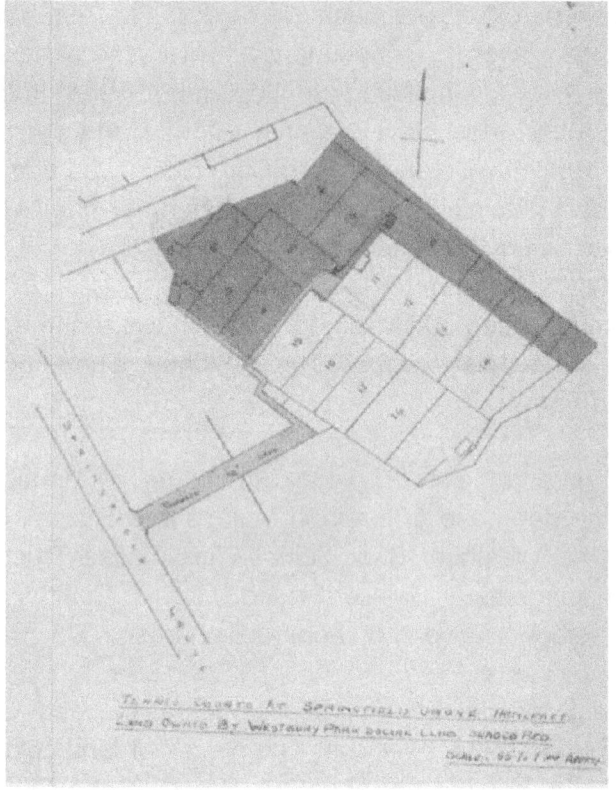

1920s – PLOTS OF LAND AVAILABLE FOR PURCHASE

During the 1920s four tennis clubs purchased courts in the Russell Grove area from Sidney Curtis:

The tennis section of Westbury Park Social Club.

Henleaze Lawn Tennis Club for URC/Henleaze Congregational Church members.

Trinity Presbyterian Lawn Tennis Club for the church originally in Cranbrook Road.

David Thomas Memorial Tennis Club. In memory of Rev David Thomas from Highbury Chapel, Cotham, founded in 1843, was its patriarchal first minister.

1922 – THE FIRST KNOWN PHOTO OF WESTBURY PARK TENNIS CLUB MEMBERS

The Club started with two tennis courts. However, by 1937 they had four grass courts and two hard courts plus a groundsman. Westbury Park Tennis Club was, at that stage, one of the largest private clubs in Bristol.

1937 – SHOWING CANON VINING WITH TENNIS CLUB MEMBERS CELEBRATING THE PURCHASE OF THE HARD COURTS

The Club was kept going through WW11 by a band of enthusiasts in tandem with their multifarious wartime activities. In April 1945 the first post-war AGM was held. Plans were agreed to welcome ex-Servicemen back from the Forces. The purchase the local Old King Street Tennis courts followed and were put into action in early 1946.

Although this has not been confirmed, it appears that the tennis section, at its peak, may have had twelve courts, some grass and some hard, and a full-time groundsman. During the early 1950s Westbury Park Social's Club membership appears to have reached 300. The club was very interactive – actors in the plays on Saturday evenings had often played tennis during the afternoon. We don't know why some of the courts were sold off, we assume they became unaffordable.

So, in order to keep going the Tennis Club going as membership decreased from the late 1950s, it is likely that WPSC and other Clubs who owned courts in Russell Grove sold the land to developers who wanted to build a road extension and 13 new homes.

An application dated August 1961 was submitted by the Westbury Park Social Club for outline planning permission of a hall for the performances of plays, dances, socials etc and incorporating changing rooms and pavilion on two alternative sites off Russell Grove and Tennessee Grove. This was not pursued, possibly because at this time of falling membership and the offer from a developer to purchase some of their land for new housing.

In April 1970 a detailed booklet was produced by Ken Badger to celebrate Westbury Park Social Club's Golden Jubilee. It highlighted the wide range of activities that the Club offered over the years which included Badminton, Billiards, Bridge, Dances, Drama, Music, Outings, Rambles, Socials, Table Tennis, Whist Drives and of course Tennis. The indoor activities held at St Alban's Hall were discontinued from 1946 owing to the shortage of halls in the City after WW11. Fortunately, Westbury Park Social Club were able to continue the majority of their indoor activities in Westmoreland Hall, off Redland Road.

The booklet also highlighted many of the active members who, over many years, had kept the club interesting and appealing to a wide sector of the community, particularly ex-servicemen and their families.

Westbury Park Social Club were proud of the continued interest and enthusiasm by its founder Canon Vining that started in 1920 and continued until his death in 1955. He had left Bristol in 1938 for Africa and by 1951 had become the First Archbishop of West Africa. Sadly, he died at sea on his way to England on 4 March 1955. He is buried in Freetown Sierra Leone.

16 JULY, 1989 – COMPETITION DAY AT THE CLUB

This new pavilion was built in the mid-1970s and is still widely used.

When Patrick Dean joined the Club c1992, only the Drama and Tennis sections were left of Westbury Park Social Club. All the other sections, whist etc, had fallen by the wayside. The Drama group used to rehearse in the Clubhouse in Russell Grove, but the actual performances were elsewhere.

Now, in 2018 there are only two tennis clubs in existence in Russell Grove – Westbury Park Tennis Club and Henleaze Lawn Tennis Club. The remaining land was utilised from the 1960s for 13 new houses plus a road extension to Russell Grove to give access to these properties.

Westbury Park Social Club is still going today, although only the tennis section remains active as Westbury Park Tennis Club; they are still in Russell Grove, and are looking forward to their 100th anniversary in 2020.

Many thanks also to Patrick Dean, Secretary of Westbury Park Tennis Club for allowing access to their archives. Here is a link to the Club who welcome new members whatever their level of tennis skills. **http://www.westburyparktennisclub.co.uk/**

∧∧∧∧∧∧∧∧∧∧∧∧∧∧∧∧∧∧∧∧∧∧∧∧∧∧∧∧∧∧∧∧∧

CHAPTER 4 – BUSINESSES

WHITE TREE GARAGE

DOROTHY BOWKER

In 2017 the Henleaze Book received an email from Lynda Gullis:

'When we lived in St Anne's my Mum Dorothy Bowkett caught a bus to White Tree roundabout before taking a short walk along North View to her work for a coach company on the junction of Northumbria Drive to where Waitrose now stands.

'Dorothy recalled there was a bank on the corner along the route she took from the White Tree to her work where a robbery had taken place.'

This had in fact occurred on 13 March 1950 at Lloyds Bank, 1 North View where several bystanders, including Robert Taylor, tried to thwart the escape of the two robbers. Sadly, Robert was shot and died. He was awarded the George Cross posthumously.

Dorothy used to take bookings for continental holidays with Wessex Coaches during the late 1940s and early 1950s at the White Tree Garage. The garage situated at the junction of North View and Northumbria Drive in Henleaze, was one of the first places in Bristol to take bookings for Continental coach tours after WWII.

Dorothy left in mid 1950s to start a family. The photo from Lynda of her Mum was taken at around the time she worked at the White Tree Garage. Dorothy died in 2005.

C1960S – WHITE TREE GARAGE

See payment booth outside the front entrance of White Tree Garage as well as the142 bus stop and the original Orpheus Cinema on Northumbria Drive. (Photo of the garage courtesy of Barry Toogood)

Some of this information appeared in the January, 2018 edition free Henleaze Book email newsletter.

∧∧∧∧∧∧∧∧∧∧∧∧∧∧∧∧∧∧∧∧∧∧∧∧∧∧∧∧∧∧∧∧

Westbury Coaches

'Mr HFD Bush (T/A Westbury Coaches) started up in 1947 in private hire at Central Garage, Clevedon and Whiteladies Road, Bristol.

In the late 1940s Mr HFD Bush purchased three Bedford coaches..

In February 1948 he was joined by A O Binding and WA Emery at these two locations.

In April 1948 the company became HFD Bush Ltd (T/A Westbury Coaches) at these locations.

In July 1948 the addresses for the company had changed to Canford Lane, Westbury-on-Trym and White Tree Garage.

From 1950 – 1952 as Westbury Luxury Coaches Ltd he purchased 11 coaches - eight of them were new. The coaches were engaged on tours to Spain, the French Riviera, Monte Carlo and Switzerland.

After May 1951 the company was known as Westbury Luxury Coaches (1952) Ltd at Canford Lane and White Tree Garage. The directors of this family run business were Bristolian Mr H F D Bush and his wife.

In the early 1950s the amount of cash that Continental tourists were allowed to take with them was progressively reduced, because of the poor balance of payments state in post-war Britain, particularly at the time of the Korean War. This meant that the continued operation of Continental coach tours became less profitable and a newly established company such as Westbury Coaches, however well run, was always going to struggle against the larger better-known giants such as Barton Transport, Wallace Arnold and Shearing's Tours.

The company took the decision to close down before the start of the 1952 season in March 1952.

WESTBURY COACHES

This photo, courtesy of Peter Tulloch from the Foden Society archives, is taken from Northumbria Drive looking down White Tree Road towards Fallodon Way. Maggs & Allen, Estate Agents, are now located on the other side of the pavement to the right on the front bus of this photo.

COVER OF COLIN MARTIN'S AND GEOFF BRUCE'S BOOK

Together they produced this really informative book on coaches which is still available on AMAZON: **http://amzn.eu/56b0rE8**

Our thanks to:

Lynda Gullis who emailed initially in 2017 asking for further information about her mother, Dorothy Bowker's work in Henleaze in the late 1940s/early 1950s,

Peter Tulloch from the bus and coach archives of the Foden Society for providing the background on Westbury Coaches,

Richard Anne Hodgson, a member of Facebook's Then and Now Photos Bristol for additional Westbury Coaches information,

Peter Davey for the photo of the two buses in White Tree Road which are in the Davey collection,

Colin Martin for providing details of the publication which he produced with Geoff Bruce, and Barry Toogood for providing some historic photos of the White Tree Garage.

Sylvia, Barry's grandmother, fulfilled the role of company secretary for the garage from the 1950s until the 1970s. She remarried and became Sylvia Vincent. Her second husband, Joe Vincent was also in the motor trade/coaches etc. and owned Severn Valley motors in Avonmouth. Although not a blood relation the owner, Bert Snelgrove remained a close personal friend of Sylvia's after his retirement in the 1970s.

^^^^^^^^^^^^^^^^^^^^^^^^^^^^^^^^^^^^^

The man with the limp

C1960s WHITE TREE GARAGE (PHOTO COURTESY OF BARRY TOOGOOD)

Feedback from past resident, Peter Northey – "I enjoyed seeing the photo of White Tree Garage taken in Northumbria Drive that featured in the December, 2017 edition of Henleaze Book email newsletter.'

'My father bought his first car from the garage car sales in early 1966. It was a grey Austin Cambridge A55, very much like the one pictured on the group of cars on the forecourt. I was wondering if the one pictured was the car that my father bought. I can't quite make out the registration number as the picture is quite grainy. I don't know if the original photo is clearer?

'The registration number of Dad's car was 605 KHU.

'My dad used to get his petrol at the garage, which in those days was a Regent garage. The pumps were on the North View side of the site and were attended by a really friendly chap, who unfortunately, walked with a limp. He always greeted us, as children, with a smile and a wave as we went by. He sat in a small booth on the lower corner of the site when he was not serving at the White Tree Garage in the 1960s.

EDITOR'S REPLY: It was interesting to receive this feedback on the White Tree Garage. Unfortunately, I do not have the original colour photo and nor does the person who sent it to me. We believe it was been lost in the fullness of time. We have tried various ways to see the registration number of the grey Austin Cambridge car but no luck I am afraid.

We hope that one of our readers can help either with their memories of the pump attendant with a limp and/or a photo using better equipment to show the number plate of the Austin Cambridge A55?

∧∧∧∧∧∧∧∧∧∧∧∧∧∧∧∧∧∧∧∧∧∧∧∧∧∧∧∧∧∧∧∧∧

MORE INFORMATION

If you have enjoyed this book here is some information on other publications produced by Veronica Bowerman which may interest you?

COVERS OF THE FOLLOWING PUBLICATIONS PRODUCED BY VERONICA BOWERMAN

Details of Veronica's books can be found at this link:

https://www.amazon.co.uk/Veronica-Bowerman/e/B001JS6O7U

The website for The Henleaze Book is:

https://www.henleazebook.com/

If you would like to be alerted of free book promotions and learn more about the area join Veronica's community by subscribing to her free monthly e-newsletter on this link:
https://my.sendinblue.com/users/subscribe/js_id/2yqf0/id/1
There is a short form to complete to comply with GDPR. You can unsubscribe at any time.

CAN YOU HELP PLEASE? Veronica would really appreciate a review on any of her books that you have read.

Every review, however short, really helps her to continue writing. Here is the link which she hopes will encourage you to do so: **https://www.amazon.co.uk/l/B001JS6O7U**

∧∧∧∧∧∧∧∧∧∧∧∧∧∧∧∧∧∧∧∧∧∧∧∧∧∧∧∧∧

ABOUT THE AUTHOR

Veronica Bowerman was born in Keynsham. In the early 1980s, she started writing local history articles on a voluntary basis for the newsletter of her local amenity society in Bristol. Although she had hated history at school, she subsequently found that she enjoyed talking to people about their memories, viewing their old photographs, many from private family collections and also researching information from the internet, local libraries and Bristol archives.

Fast forward 10 years to 1991, when she produced the first local and social history book solely dedicated to the suburb of Henleaze, Bristol entitled THE HENLEAZE BOOK. This was followed by much larger second edition in 2006.

On retirement, after nearly 40 years of living in Henleaze she and her husband, Jim moved to North Somerset near Weston super Mare. Since moving Veronica has produced a further six books, four on Henleaze and two on travel.

Two free heritage trails for Henleaze and Westbury-on-Trym are available in pdf format.

Printed in Dunstable, United Kingdom

65495768R00090